FROM
NIGER
TO THE
N WORD

TONY DEVAUN MCNEIL

Paperback: 978-1-958381-22-9
eBook: 978-1-958381-18-2
Library of Congress Control Number: 2024903625

This is a work of nonfiction.

SWEETSPIRE LITERATURE
—— MANAGEMENT ——

This book is dedicated to El Hajj Malik El Shabaaz, also known as Malcolm X. This work is not for the memory of the fiery misguided minister of the Nation of Islam, but for the awakened Human Rights Leader who wanted goodwill for all of humanity, without regard to the color of skin.

CONTENTS

INTRODUCTION

The purpose of this book is to offer some solutions to the problem of race relations in America. For the Black reader, the existence of race problems is no revelation, for they have experienced them first-hand. Many White readers will meet the problem with feigned disbelief and some with defensive anger. Feigned disbelief, because many Whites say to us, "It's not like that anymore."

It is not my intention to use injustices as a crutch, to justify doing less than my/our best. Neither is it my goal to demand anything that we do not deserve. No matter what others think of me, I will strive to achieve a higher standard in all that I do. What qualifies me to write this book? I am qualified because I am a Black man, living in America, with "opened eyes." I have received my degree in race relations from "the school of hard knocks." That school demanded that I take certain classes, but it also offered electives. The electives included love, compassion, and fellowship, which I have been blessed to share with many White people over the years.

Black people today and the nonwhites of the past are all joined by a history more powerful than mere words could express. This is true, which means whether you understand it or not, does not diminish its reality. The legacy of Black people in America cannot be discarded, and the "blood of the Black men and women cries out from the ground of America!" PS: Make notes and feel free to contact me with your suggestions for making the world and us better.

CHAPTER ONE

Definitions

In July of 1997, I was stationed at Fort Carson, Colorado, with the US Army, where I wrote for an independent newspaper called The African-American Voice. In my column called My Two Cents I continually called on Black people to rise up mentally, and strive to live out their/our potential as men and women. I found myself defending one of my columns when my White Company Commander felt I wrote negatively and specifically about him. In that issue, I addressed some points of the late Human Rights leader, Malcolm X. I pointed out how (racist) White people take our words out of context and make it look like were something we really are not. In response to my column, my White commander took my words out of context and verbally reprimanded me for what I had written. In the course of our discussion, he accused me of hiding behind words and twisting them to suit my own purposes.

"Sir, I use words in their correct meanings. It is you, who use words incorrectly, I pointed out to him."

He did not want to hear that any more than the average person on the street wants to hear it. That he would not hear it did not negate its existence. English, or more correctly, American may be an easy language to learn, compared to other exotic languages such as Chinese, Hungarian, and Native American, or so it seems. One of the problems with the American language though, is the multiplicity of meanings for words. The secondary meanings that were originally incorrect become so much a part of American speech that it can be difficult to resist using them improperly. For this reason, vocabulary becomes a hindrance to meaningful dialogue. African-Americans for example have become so adept at speaking in a way that keeps passersby from understanding that White people have begun to believe we speak a different language, Ebonics. The words spoken mean one thing, but in context, familiar words take on completely different meanings. Still different from so-called Ebonics or slang, are simple inflections in tone, which give clearer meaning to the listeners. For the sake of clarity, I have defined some of the terms I will be using throughout this book:

BLACK (people)

In this book, Black refers to all persons in the world that are not direct descendants of European-Caucasian.

I always get a kick out of Caucasian people who will admit that Jesus the Christ was not European-Caucasian (White), but will not say, "He was Black!"

"No, he was not White, but I would not say he was Black, they say. Some correctly compare Him to the Jewish people found in the Middle East today, but still insist that he was not Black. Perhaps they have a different meaning when the say Black that we have not been aware of. Their unwillingness to accept a Black savior seems to betray their subconscious prejudices.

CAUCASIAN (people)

This term sometimes applied to a broad and increasingly vague subdivision of the human species with a predominance of light skin color and higher percentages of light-colored eyes and hair than are found in other segments of the population. The designation Caucasian was first used in the 19th and early 20th centuries by scholars who believed that this subdivision of humankind originated in Caucasia, or around the Caucus mountains, a region of southeastern Europe. Caucasians are now more commonly known as the White race.

Europe is usually considered the center White population and America, even though the spread of Caucasians into North and South America began only a few centuries ago. Hundreds of millions of people in India and the Middle East, however, are most frequently classified as Caucasoid peoples, in areas where distinctions are not clear between White and nonwhite populations.

In North America, confusion over the designation White or Caucasian is considerable. Many people, including Puerto Ricans and Mexican-Americans, are now being identified as Hispanic rather than White in social counts of American populations, such as the United States Census. Increasingly, the term White is becoming a residual category, denoting that part of the population not covered by the following classifications: Blacks, Hispanics, East Asians, Native Americans, Pacific Islanders, and other racial subdivisions.

COLORED

According to Webster's New World Dictionary, all of humankind, that is not Caucasian, or White. In South Africa, a colored person is one of racially mixed parentage, usually spelled c-o-l-o-u-r-e-d. It is also defined as altered, distorted, or exaggerated. If colored means altered or distorted, then off-colored jokes must then be unaltered, undistorted, unexaggerated, and the norm, or color is acceptable and normal.

CRIMINALIZATION

Malcolm X described it as the systematic portrayal of a person or class of people as criminals. Unfortunately, many African-Americans try to live up to this stereotype, often due to the influence of Rap artists. Today we see young Black men attempting to prove their Blackness by walking like their leg is broken, talking like their tongue is broken, and acting like their mind is broken.

Abolitionist, Frederick Douglass said, "Where justice is denied, where poverty is enforced, where ignorance prevails, and where any, one class is made to feel that society is in an organized conspiracy to oppress, rob, and degrade them, neither persons nor property will be safe."

While looking down the halls of history, it becomes clear that people have been put into situations where they wrongly come to believe they have no choice but to resort to crime as a source of income. Justifying evil, this is wrong, spiritually damning, and possibly the cause for loss of freedom or life. There are many avenues to financial help other than crime. I do not blame crime on anyone but the criminal who, of his own free will, chooses to commit a crime. I do blame the propulsion of drugs into nonwhite communities on someone other than the nonwhite fools who poison their own people in the name of money. If there were no market for illegal drugs, no one sends or brings them into our communities. No Black person at any degree of poverty is forced to sell drugs, even when the instigator of such trafficking manipulates or take advantage of the environment that is so conducive to pushing drugs.

I blame the media directly and the government indirectly, for constantly portraying Blacks as criminals, disingenuously proportionate to White criminals. Presently, Black people are charged under the Three Strikes Law seven times more than Whites are. Is this just a coincidence?

NIGGA

Different from the word nigger, NIGGA is used both as slang for friend, fellow African-American, or enemy. For example, one African-American may say to another, "What's up my nigga?" While on the other hand speak in a degrading manner, "Man, I'm gonna bust a cap in that nigga!"

The term has become so heavily used in both positive and negative connotations that it is no longer a sensitive point to many Blacks. Many White people fail to realize that this term is not nigger, and because of the context, correct inflection in voice, and relationship to the person with whom he uses the term, it is clearly understood to be positive or negative. If a White person uses the term, it is not as clear what his meaning is unless he is speaking to a Black person he is very close. I do agree with those who espouse that the term should not be used under any circumstances.

NIGGARD

This word was added to the English language to cushion the word nigger. This new word means a stingy, miserly person with no reference to skin color. This word could not have been used to describe Black slaves, since they had nothing with which to be stingy! I surprised my commander when I presented for him, the true definition of the word that was used, via my older version of The Standard Dictionary. The word Nigger, not Niggard.

My commander tried to justify the use of the word nigger by a White soldier referenced to a Black soldier. This ploy was obvious because, the commander was not present to hear the context or tone of voice used. How could he even attempt it, knowing that he was not present, that it was I who verbally witnessed the deed? Also, a friend of that soldier using the word nigger later confided in me that the user was in fact racist.

NIGGER

Offensive Slang. a. Used as a disparaging term for a Black person. b. Used as a disparaging term for a member of any dark-skinned people. 2. Used as a disparaging term for a member of any socially, economically, or politically deprived group of people. [Alteration of dialectal neger, black person, from French negre, from Spanish Negro. See Negro.]

Though I cannot judge their rationale for it, I have heard some White people assert that, "a nigger can be either Black or White." I asked (not begged) their pardon, and explained that the term did not originated to describe Black people and is not synonymous with anything other than people. What person honestly visualizes a White person when they hear the term nigger being used?

Even in the SI-SA Elite English / Dictionary the following words are defined:

NIGGER-1. Negro, 2. Black person

NIGGERHEAD-Negrohead

NIGGER IN THE WOOD PILE-hidden fact

In the Word Perfect word processing system, it is referred to as an offensive term. The ugly term followed White US soldiers to Iraq and Iran, where the native people to that area were referred to as "Sand Niggers."

This word meant Black, without regard to social status, economic status, or education. I have often wondered about the origin of the term "nigger." It appears that ignorant slave traders mispronounced the land of Niger as Nigger. I can imagine an uneducated, southern person of the 1800's using such a term. I remember a Drill sergeant from Fort Jackson, South Carolina that used the word "Private," as a put down. The word Private actually refers to the first three ranks in the US Army: Private E-1, Private E-2, and Private First Class. The tone used by this particular Drill Sergeant, i.e. "Come here 'Private,'" placing the type of emphasis on the term Private to make sound like a put down.

RACE

Though defined diversely in dictionaries and encyclopedias, "race" is just another word for color. No matter where one finds his roots, if his skin is White, as in European-Caucasoid, he is pinkish to pasty white. Whether it is admitted by Whites or not, every person, whose skin is not white, is considered to be Black. Along with all people whose skin is brown with Afro-centric features, persons who are clearly nonwhite can be considered Black. The reality of color is that all of humanity falls into one of three categories: Either all of humanity is Black with shades as dark as Black/blue and as light as White. Everyone is White with shades as light as White and as dark as Black/blue. The only third option is that there are two separate and distinct races, or color classifications. One classification is Black, and the other White.

The evidence for a singular race lies in the fact that no dividing line of so-called different races holds true across the board. According to encyclopedias, race cannot be defined by a person's skin color, features, ethnicity, or place of birth. "So-called," because there are Caucasians that are just as Black as Negroes, just as there are Spanish-Americans that look just as white or pink as Caucasians.

People are divided into different races, to classify them and the White scientist, who came up with the classifications of five major races, pronounced the Caucasoid the superior among them. The only justification they could find for their superiority was their Whiteness. It seems the point of the Islamic parable of Ibliss spelled out in chapter 12, has some basis in the reality of a sick mind. Many Whites fail to accept the fact that they are not the authors of all of the sciences, arts, or schools of thought. Much of what they gained was stolen or adopted from nonwhite people, from spaghetti to fireworks. Ironically, one of the sciences they can lay some claim to, is Egyptology, the study of the Black people known as Egyptians and their history. If Black scholars and archeologists were at the front of Egyptology, the full truth might be known. It matters what color the Egyptians were because their Blackness destroys the White superiority ideology. How could intellectually disadvantaged people create magnificent works which White people today still cannot duplicate? Black people built the pyramids and made paint that lasted thousands of years, when the paint that we have today barely lasts a hundred years.

RACIAL DISCRIMINATION

The dominant (White) races acting out on feelings of bias toward nonwhite people. Racial discrimination from nonwhite people is not possible because the so-called minorities generally do not have the power to enforce racial bias. There are now exceptions to this rule because minorities (nonwhites) have been able to move into a few places of power. In these exceptional cases, the nonwhite can be guilty of reverse racial discrimination.

Racial discrimination is often defined as the feeling of superiority by the controlling race over the minority race. With this as the main characteristic of racism, ask yourself, "Who is considered the controlling race?" Because relatively few nonwhite people are in positions of power, most can't, by definition, be guilty of racial discrimination! Certainly, Black people can hate White people, but hate in and of itself, is not racial discrimination, as we understand it. Minorities need not apologize for the dictionary definitions, because we did not write the dictionary. As far as hatred itself goes, Jose Mari Perez said in The Manifesto of Monte Cristo, "Only those who hate the Negro see hatred in the Negro."

RACISM

The false belief that race is the primary determinant of human traits and capacities. That "racial" differences produce an inherent superiority of a particular race. Racial prejudice or discrimination.

RACIST

Originally defined as a White person that holds a bias against nonwhites, today racists are defined as any person that holds a bias against someone because of untrue stereotypical beliefs about them as members of another race. Modern lexicographers are now saying any person can be a racist, but we still use the word "reverse racism" in reference to a nonwhite person who is racially biased against a White person. The terms reverse racist and reverse racism are used to describe nonwhites who show hatred or bias against White people. This seems to declare that the origin of hatred of one race against the other began with the hatred of nonwhites by whites. To say, you can be any color and be a racist, shows ignorance of the words original meaning.

No matter how brutish, inhumane, or animalistic a person may act, no human can actually be a racist, because there is only one race of mankind: human! Since it would be madness to be against the human race in which we are all a part of we find something different about our fellow humans to focus our hate.

I say if the hate for nonwhite people is based on justifiable precepts, rather than rejecting us, lets change that which is abhorrent about us. Then there would be no reason to hate or reject us and we can do our share to end racism! The answers must, though, be honest, justifiable, and true. If the answer given in The Book of Mormon, at Jacob 3:5 is accurate, then there is nothing Black people can ever do to be loved and accepted by racist Whites.

"Behold the Lamanites your brethren, whom ye hate because of their filthiness and the cursing which hath come upon their skins." As expounded on in chapter three, Mormons are lead to believe beautiful White people were turned Black, stupid, mischievous, and deceitful.

STEREOTYPE

Exaggerated belief associated with a category. Its function is to justify our conduct in relation to that category. Exaggerated, untrue beliefs about someone or something based on accepted ideas that are not true.

WHITE (people)

Regarding race relations, and specifically racism, White is usually used to refer to those Caucasian people that in some way express their racist feelings. For example, if I said, White people were deceitful in their dealings with the Native Americans. I of course, would not mean literally all White people. I would be speaking of those who were in fact, guilty of the acts to which I was referring.

Using White in this way is different, though Caucasian people who hear the term being used often misunderstand it. They are quick to defend themselves, pointing out that they have never owned any slaves. Of course they have not, but they assuredly act just like the former slave owners. Hence, they cannot so easily sever the ties that bind, except they repent (change). They must change from their thinking that they are better simply because of their Whiteness. They must change from thinking anyone that is not European-Caucasian is less than they are. They must learn to love, live in harmony with nonwhites, and they become upright and deal in justice.

The dominant race has to be divided and made to believe they are the minority, and therefore beneath the supposed majority. The thought of all Black (nonwhite) people united politically economically and socially scares White supremacists! It would scare them more if there were any likelihood of complete unity of the nonwhite masses. The White supremacist knows that he is only supreme because too many Black people are not striving for greatness. Too many are content just getting by, and that automatically elevates those who want more out of life. We, Black people make the White man supreme ourselves, by acting in a subordinate manner. Were the house slaves and field slaves at odds with each another? It has been accepted that the two types of slaves, the field slave, and the house slave. This is true; the questionable aspect is the idea that there was friction between these two groups of slaves. I don't know how far reaching this may have been. I do know that there have been slave revolts, stopped only because one of the house slaves revealed the plot. This would obviously cause distrust, and animosity. The point is that both sides were slaves, and they should have drawn on that as a point of unity. Many times though, their own self-interests caused them to be at odds. The field slave may have been envious of the easier life of the house slave. At the same time the house slaves were known to disclose plans for revolt among the field slaves. Today we likewise, should also draw upon what we have in common, rather than attempting to destroy each other. Foolish Rappers, battling East Coast against West Coast when neither coast belongs to either of them.

Imagine if nonwhite people Awoke up, realizing our common Blackness and united based on what we have in common. As Malcolm X pointed out, "What we have most in common is our color." Imagine all nonwhites united socially, politically, economically, and even spiritual. We could use our united power to change the direction of the world! Since nonwhites have always been quick to love and forgive Whites, the world would be a better place with the new rulers. Unfortunately, while Whites need to learn to love us, we as nonwhites still have to work on loving each other.

In war, divide and conquer has always been a good strategy, and as long as nonwhites are divided and some even trying to pretend they are White, the minority (Whites) rules the majority (nonwhite). I say nonwhite because I know that some Spanish, Asian, and Mexican-Americans may take offense to being called Black. Is it because they are not aware of the fact that they are indeed Black? Is possible that they have so much pride in their specific heritage that they want to be identified especially with that heritage? Perhaps, like some other Black people, they too, actually want to be White? I once watched a documentary, where an Asian male went so far as to have his eyes surgically altered to make them more western.

CHAPTER TWO

Justifiable Racism

It is too easy to say, "I hate all of them." It becomes difficult to honestly justify that hate. One could more easily justify hating the actions of a person or people. One may even hate the attitudes of others, but it is much more difficult to honestly justify hating another person, much less a whole, group, class, or race of people.

Hatred of an entire class of people cannot be honestly justified because no complete mass of people is deserving of being abhorred, despised, detested, or loathed. For White slave-owners, there had to be Blacks along the road to slavery that made ownership of Black people possible. Moreover, one cannot easily justify enmity, malice, or malignity between the two classes of people that we commonly refer to as Black and White, without any knowledge of history.

Beyond slavery in America, there is a history that holds the answers to why some White people hate Black people. Why have so many White people found it easy to hate nonwhites, while nonwhites find it just as easy to love and forgive them? Lost is the truth about hatred so deep that it seems to be passed on from generation to generation. Like eyes, ears, hair color, it appears that racism can be genetically passed from parent to child. My two-month-old daughter sleeps in the same position as I do. She holds her hand alongside her cheek as I do, and prefers to have her eyes covered when she goes to sleep as I do. These similarities between a thirty-four-year-old father and his two-month-old daughter cannot be simple coincidence. Neither can they be learned, since she has not been able to watch me close enough to mimic my actions as I sleep.

When confronted with this raw candor, many White people cannot suppress their feelings. We cannot be so naive that we believe that this type of hatred began with the institution of slavery in America. Racism runs too deep and is too strong for such a relatively limited time span. Some of the friendliest White people I have met become very uncomfortable when confronted with the truth about them. Watch them if you get into a deep conversation about the origins of racism, the color of Jesus, or the undeniable hypocrisy and injustice in religion, law, and the judicial system. If they do not get uncomfortable in your presence, try to get them to state their views in front of several other White people. I do not really want anyone to do something that would endanger peace, but I do want to make a strong point.

Some Blacks merely hate White people because White people hate Black people. On the other hand, some White people hate Black people simply because some Blacks hate Whites. This foolish cycle had to start with one hating the other first! Rather than ponder who started it, I challenge Whites to love nonwhites, giving us time to see their sincerity, then watch as the day that Dr. King dreamed of comes into view. White people have the duty to love us today because we have always loved them!

White explorers were accepted by the nonwhites (Black people) that they came in contact with, but these same Indians, Africans, Aztecs, etc. who helped, were hated in return. They were called savages, and in return for acceptance of the Whites, they were lied to, murdered, treated savagely, and enslaved.

Visualize a young Black boy (Malcolm Little) in 1930's Nebraska. Malcolm, the only Black child in his class is asked, along with his classmates, what he wanted to be when he grew up. Malcolm proclaims proudly that he wants to be a lawyer. Rather than encourage the child to keep his dreams, the teacher tells Malcolm to Abe a realistic nigger, that he should do something with his hands, such as carpentry. The child grows to manhood with an ever-increasing, pessimistic perception of evil, all White people who enter his life. Would history have recorded a great Black lawyer named Malcolm little, instead of the fiery minister of the Nation of Islam known as Malcolm X?

Just as Malcolm X reacted to the racism from White people, perhaps White people have reacted to some long forgotten evil deed or deeds of Black people. Perhaps the hatred of Blacks by some White people is based, not on the color our skin, but some long forgotten evil we are guilty of inflicting on them. This is more realistic since hating any human being because his skin is a different color has to be the epitome of asininity!

Today the image of young Black men is so vile that I, myself a Black man, sometimes react cautiously when I meet a young brother. What's worse though, is the fact that too many young Black men turn to violence and law breaking, thereby supporting the justification of profiling based on a racial stereotype. If I as a Black man have to consciously fight stereotypes that I know to be wrong, what can we expect from the White person who may not accept that the stereotype is untrue. Wouldn't it be great if no Black man committed any crime, or injustice toward anyone else, especially another Black man? Wouldn't it be good if it were not so easy for police officer's killing of a Black man, to be labeled Justifiable Homicide?

Racism in the police forces with the stereotyping of Black men as criminals leads to the hating and killing of Black men, and Black people in general. Who could be expected to regret removing a no-good person from the world, no-good, and a nigger? Once the justification is in place, injustices toward Black people no longer bother their consciences because to them, the end justifies the means. One thinks, "Well, he was probably guilty anyway. If not for this for something else, he has gotten away with."

Justifiable racism is the use of racist stereotyping to justify hating other people. Not all Black men are criminals, and not all Black women are on Welfare, rejecting chances to get a job. If a reason is given for the hatred, then the hate continues. Therefore, if we destroy the justification, it is conceivable that we could end racism!

I have met White soldiers who have confessed that they had never seen a Black person in real life until they joined the Army. They learned that Black people are simply people who are Black. Truth is very powerful when one realizes that many people harboring racist feelings do so because they are ignorant of the very class of people they hate. When my mother-in-law got to know me as a person, and not a stereotype of Black people, not one of them, but a decent human being, she was able to love me.

CHAPTER THREE

Institutional Racism

The idea of any institution as a whole, condoning or promoting racism in this modern era seems improbable . . . for those who are not affected by it. On one side, nonwhites seem to be kept out of institutions; while on the other hand, those that make it in through affirmative action are branded as less than qualified. The idea that a Black person can steal a job from a qualified White person is as ridiculous as totally justifying our own lack of achievement on White people. The Man may in fact be attempting to stop Black achievement, but no one can keep us down for long if we never give up. If we put our heads together, and use knowledge wisely, no one can stop us from achieving anything we set our minds to. It is recorded in the Bible at Genesis 1:6 that at the Tower of Babel that God said that if men put their minds together, there is nothing that we could not accomplish. We can see here that men can be united for evil, even for something as seemingly trite such as pride. The Tower of Babel was an example of what happens when pride is the motivating factor. Imagine the evil that is perpetrated in the name of the all mighty dollar. Not money itself, but the love of money is the root of <u>all sorts</u> of evil, I Timothy 6:10.

The irony of institutional racism is that true to the law of physics it spawned Affirmative Action as the opposite reaction. Well look at affirmative action in greater detail in chapter nine.

Most institutions are headed, owned, and run predominantly by White people, so it is easy to assume institutional racism exists. We must be careful though, to not assume that everything that looks like racism is racism. There is evidence of institutional racism:

<u>BUSINESS</u>

After lawsuits for denying service to African-Americans were leveled against them, Denny's Restaurant chain then began to run infomercials claiming a percentage of Black owned franchises. That's the same as saying, "I'm not racist, I have a Black friend." Some White people actually think Blacks are so stupid that today they can still make the same comments they made in 1920, 1940, 1950, and 1960. Words and phrases like responsible and for a Black person, are still used with the same meaning even if the racist is no longer overt in his thinking. Famous Western movie actor John Wayne once said, "I believe in white supremacy until the blacks are educated to a point of responsibility."

In all honesty, I am not sure what he meant by that, but if he meant nonwhites debase themselves by "niggerly" actions and attitudes, I can't argue with him. If on the other hand he like, the Whites of his day, mean that Blacks have to go beyond what Whites will allow them in order to prove their humanity, then his soul is not resting where it now.

POLITICS

In 1990 The National Opinion Research Center reported its findings that only 11% of persons polled would vote for a Black presidential candidate whether he was qualified or not! Ask Jessie Jackson how he felt when he was forced to denounce Louis Farrakhan before the biggest political gathering of the year. During the Presidential campaigns of 1984 much of America came first heard of Nation of Islam (NOI) Minister, Louis Farrakhan. He had come forward to endorse Reverend Jessie Jackson for the Democratic Party's nomination, only to be used as a tool against Jackson.

RELIGION

Was it revelation or progress in the Civil Rights movement those lead Mormon leaders to allow Black men to hold office in the Mormon Church? Will they divine guidance to change "The Book of Mormon," which states that beautiful White people were turned Black, stupid, and mischievous? Perhaps people accept it because it's what they already want to believe before hearing such ridiculous propaganda in the name of religion. Too bad they did not hold Gods command not to make new religions so enthusiastically.

CHAPTER FOUR

Can We Afford you?

In the movie, A Soldier Story, set in the days just prior to WWII, A Black Sergeant tells a Black Private that because he exhibits some of the negative, Black stereotypes, Black people can't afford him anymore. The Sergeant further explained that White officers could not take Black soldiers serious as long as they acted like "grinning house niggers," only interested in acting a fool in front of the "massa."

In a like manner, Blacks today who want to be accepted as human beings with the same potential as anyone else cannot afford "niggers" who put a blemish on all people of color. When they degrade themselves before the White masses and give justification for their feelings of superiority, we say to the hirer, don't hire me. We say to the lending institution, don't approve my loan application. We say to the religious leaders, continue to mislead me. We open the door to be exploited and ostracized by the very people that have the positions of power over us. If you don't think you are subordinate to the White power structure, get the things you need in life without the aid or acceptance of White people along the way. The truth is that we do need them, just as assuredly as they do not need us. They can hire someone else to the work for them, or purchase their products and services, but whom could we go to for employment, housing, and instruction in education, politics, and religion. It is not my assertion that there are no nonwhite people who will give honest wages, goods, services, or instruction, as it is neither my assertion that all White people won't. I am saying that the majority of the leadership in any field is White. Until we have our own, we must placate them at one time or another.

Use the template bellow to perform an analysis of yourself, then answer whether Black people can we "afford you." If your answers in the template below are negative, then you are not an asset but a liability to Black people and society as a whole. Place as many defining answers in the blanks as possible. There is no right or wrong answer, only a starting point for the honest researcher.

WHAT AM I?	WHAT DO I WANT TO BECOME?	HOW DO I WANT TO BE PERCEIVED?	HOW DO OTHERS PERCEIVE ME?

Once you have filled in the template, ask yourself, "What can I do to better myself, physically, mentally, and spiritually," then do it.

"Can you proudly and honestly proclaim, 'We declare our rights on this earth to be a man, to be a human being, to be respected as a human being in this society, on this earth, in this day which we intend to bring into existence by any means necessary?" Understand that to make that declaration is akin to saying, "I am a man, a respectable human being, and a positive part of society." To answer the sister's question, "Yes. If your husband is in jail 'just because' he bought some crack cocaine, he is a bad person." That he is bad doesn't mean he must always be bad, or that others are not equally bad, it does mean that he must repent from the bad and become righteous or return to the righteousness he once held.

"How much are you worth? If what you thought of yourself were converted to money, how much would you have?"

1. Do you own and use a library card?

God Himself declares at Hosea 4:6, "My people are destroyed for lack of knowledge." Because thou hast rejected knowledge, I will also forget thy children. Furthermore, at Proverbs 1:7 it is revealed for us that "(Reverential) fear of the Lord is the beginning of wisdom." And who has not heard that knowledge is power? The unarguable point is that since with knowledge, or wisdom, there is power, the lack of knowledge or wisdom means the lack of power. The reason most of us are downtrodden, is not because the man is holding us down. It is our lack of education keeps us down. Even when the system is against us, we can overcome it if we obtain the knowledge, which will dictate the best direction to move in achieving justice as much as personal and professional success.

2. Do you respect yourself and our women?

One definition of respect is acknowledging the status, position, or worth of someone or something. If we hold our history, ourselves, and our women in the proper places of honor and worth, we will not treat them as we do and we would not show the disrespect that we do toward and around them! If our women were important, we would not treat them as whores, use vulgarity in their presence, or abandon them when they are carrying our child.

If we respected, our history, we would strive to be more like the great Black men and women of the past. How could we reject the importance of wisdom, with the great, Black King Solomon as a role model, or the great learning institute of the world at Timbuktu, Africa? Understand that Black men of antiquity first charted the skies, built the pyramids, and sailed to America long before Columbus was born! Don't deceive yourself, or be deceived, it is paramount to remember the past. There are those who know this, and because of their vested interest in seeing us dumb, have given us a history devoid of color.

"Why was Jesus painted White?" The artist did not accept a Messiah whose features were unlike his own features. In all honesty, if I did not accept White people as my equals, I would reject a White

Messiah, just as they reject a Black Messiah. In my and most Black peoples defense, we have not only accepted a White version of the Messiah, but even with the obvious evidence that prove Jesus was Black, we, as a whole, still look to a White Jesus. Black people can accept a White Jesus, but White people get in an uproar when Jesus is correctly portrayed as Black. Ask the people of Union City, New Jersey why the ticket cancellations and death threats were leveled against African-American Desi Arnaz Giles who portrayed Jesus in "The Passion Play?" Giles pointed out that it was totally acceptable when he played Herod, who sought to kill the baby Jesus, or Lucifer in other cities.

Whites will say, "It doesn't matter what color Jesus was." What they really mean is, "It doesn't matter when his color is white." If it doesn't matter, then Whites should not reject a Black Messiah. A well-meaning white person even told me that I could win more converts to Christianity if I did not mention the fact that Jesus was Black. Imagine forfeiting your salvation because the savior is not White? It doesn't matter what color Jesus was if we look to his color to mean we are better than others of a different color are. It does matter when the truth of his color is proof that someone is conning you into sending them money based on the premise that they want to preserve the burial cloth of Jesus. When the Jesus of the shroud is a White face, it becomes a "Horse of a different color," pun intended. The Shroud of Turin, which it was claimed was the burial cloth of Jesus bears the enigmatic likeness of a man bearing the <u>artistic version</u> of the Jesus Christ, but not of the actual likeness.

Jesus of the Shroud	Jesus of the Bible
*Minor wounds.	*Flesh lacerated beyond belief. Isaiah 52:14
*Long straight hair.	*According to Jewish law, Jesus would have short hair unless he was of the sect of the Nasserite, which he was not. Bible reference to wool was color of the glorified Jesus hair. Numbers 6:5, I Corinthians 11:14-15
*Caucasian features.	*Being Hebrew, Jesus features included brown skin. Daniel 10:6, Revelation 1:15
*Attractive Male.	*The prophet Isaiah said Jesus would be unattractive when He appeared. Isaiah 53:2
*Hands are deformed.	*I have found no mention of deformities in Jesus hands.
*Very little blood.	*According to the biblical description of Jesus' crucifixion there had to be tremendous blood loss, and open wounds.

The words of the Bible declare at Galatians 3:28, "there is neither Jew (Black) nor Greek (White), there is neither bond nor free, there is neither male nor female; for ye are all one in Christ Jesus." Unfortunately most are not; neither do they seek to be "in Christ." To be in Christ calls for self-sacrifice, obedience, endurance, and righteousness, to name among other adjectives that most of today's society does not care to live up to. How many physically strong Black men want to develop those spiritual and mentally efficacious qualities? Unfortunately, not enough, and I challenge and beg you to prove me wrong that, There is neither Jew (Black) nor gentile (White), bond nor free, for ye are all one in Christ. Unfortunately most are not; neither do they seek to be in Christ. To be in Christ (a Christian) calls for self-sacrifice, obedience, endurance, and righteousness, to name a few traits. How many physically strong Black men want to develop those spiritual and mentally efficacious qualities? Unfortunately, not enough, and I challenge and beg to be proven me wrong.

3. Do your pants hang off your butt?

I have already breached the topic of appearance, and the importance of being socially acceptable. We can't afford to have White people assuming they can recognize at a glance the type of person we are, based on what we look like. Since we can't make them read our minds, we must display an acceptable (to society and good taste) appearance. We also, should not assume that others are a certain way because of the way they appear to us. We have more to lose since we typically rely on Caucasians for employment. Weigh the ramifications of one of the questions on a Police Exam, Would you shoot a Black person?

4. Do you use profanity?

A great depth of ignorance is found in a person's inability to tastefully express himself. It is this show of ignorance that can be used to depict us as sub-humans, deserving to be hated, despised, exploited, and even killed. To counter the tendency to use profanity one need only enrich his or her vocabulary. If we have a repertoire of accepted words, well no longer need little unacceptable words.

When the time comes to verbally express ourselves, we can do so in an articulate manner wherein our speech will be heard. Malcolm X was not liked by the White public in general, but because of his command of the English language they had to take note that he was not just another mad nigger. Rappers in the same manner could do away with the vulgarity that has become so common in their music. Neither do they need to preach to the choir, contending that they are merely telling it like it really is in the ghettos of America. The people that buy their music know how unpleasant life in the "hood" is. I challenge Rappers to tell us how we can unite to fix the ills of the hoods across America! They cannot reach many of the White music lovers primarily because of the language that is so offensive. It is my contention that White teenagers are now turning to "Gangsta Rap," not necessarily because of the quality of the music and its message, but as a form of rebellion. If it is because of their rebellion, then choosing Rap as a display of that rebellious attitude identifies it as something we should reject. Like drugs, it seems that the cycle of giving the public what it wants and the publics accepting what is offered is the folly of Gangsta Rap Music. Today we see rappers telling us that which we, nonwhites, already know while they should be offering solutions to the problems of the hood.

Being aware of the fact that so many Blacks are into Rap, artists can use their trade as a tool to spread the message of self-reliance and mental sanctification. Some Rap artists have the messages we need to hear, and that is good. Rappers who did not curse, and did send clean messages in their music fall by the way side. Examples include MC Hammer, Run DMC, and Grand Master Flash, etc. There was more to these artists' end than just the lack of audiences for their music, but it was only a portion.

5. Do you have dreams and goals?

It is important to have dreams and goals, because they can help guide us in practically our entire decision making. The Decision-Making Process consists of five components:

I. Identify the Problem:

Before we can do anything about any problem, we must first understand exactly what the main problem is. There can be many manifestations of a problem, but we must investigate so as not to spend time on symptoms of the problem, but the problem itself.

II. Gather Information:

What do you know about the problem? What makes it a challenge to overcome? What gives it power over you? What is the weakness of this opponent or obstacle that I can use to conquer it?

III. List Possible Courses of Action:

List the courses of action, and then prioritize them. What is within my reach to help me master this test? Who do I know that has information and/or assets that I can use to triumph over my problem(s)?

IV. Select the Best Course of Action:

Once your options are prioritized with the most likely course of action at the fore, you increase your chances of success. Rather than blindly "stabbing in the dark" you try the most likely route to success.

V. Implement and Reevaluate:

Put your ideas into action and make a vow to yourself that you will not give up until you have resolved the conflict facing you. When I put all my efforts into the best course of action, there is less chance of losing heart because of defeat suffered by not using the best choice. If you do not meet with success, you may only need to be more persistent with your first decision or attempt the next course of action on your list. When you are finally successful, then you will either gain faith in yourself, or increase your existing self-esteem. Don't give up if you are not successful on the first attempt. Consider it a short pause on your road to success.

If our dreams and goals are important enough to us, we won't jeopardize them for sex, money, drugs, etc. If we don't have dreams and goals, we are like a boat set upon the waters without a ruder. The wind blows east, and the boat goes east. The wind blows west or south, and the boat goes west or south. Our proper dreams and goals will set us down a path that will steer us away from the negative aspects of life that are not a part of our realistic dream or goal in life.

6. Do you commit crimes?

It is harder to prove a person's innocence if they have committed any crimes in the past. When Blacks commit crimes, those of us who are innocent have the burden of looking like the typical criminal to all bigoted White people. This is why we hear about police profiling. By the same token, if we are honest, we must admit that too many criminals are non-white.

This is the reason a White person can go into the average store with a Black person and steal the store blind. Store workers are so conditioned to believe that the Black patron will steal that they may not notice the real culprit. When virtually no Black person is guilty of crime, there should be no stereotyping. The good cop will not have reason to suspect Black people, and the bad cop will have no evidence of Black criminals. The sacrifice calls for the end of the type of Rap music that glorifies gangsters, thugs, criminals, killers, and such.

7. Would you want your daughter to marry someone just like yourself?

Would you want your son to grow up to be just like you? To answer these questions honestly is to come to terms with one's true nature. Most people want to see their children better off than they are or were. If you don't want to see your daughter with someone just like yourself, then you are not the man you should be. We should all do self-analysis of ourselves from time to time, and then correct any shortcomings we may find.

Psychologists state that women look for in a potential husband, what they see in their fathers. Men likewise look for in a wife, what they saw in their mothers. If this is true, don't we owe it to our children to be best mothers and fathers possible?

8. Do you have self-worth?

Self-worth means that you recognize your potential as a human being. When you have self-worth, you don't have to lower yourself to the level of sub human because "that's what they think of me anyway." This is a cop out and facilitates the racism based on your being what has been claimed of you. If you have self-worth, you will strive to improve yourself each day, even if only modestly. The most important areas are obedience to God and continuing your education beyond established learning institutes. We should frequent the libraries at least once a week. There, we should study politics, history, investing, religion, achievement and motivation.

An excellent way to bring about achievement in any given field is to study the biographies of people who have achieved great success in the field that you hope to go into. If you apply the things that worked for them and avoid the things that were not helpful to their success, you can save the time, money, and effort learning the hard way, and learn from their mistakes. As you develop the real world knowledge, versus school taught knowledge your self-esteem and personal worth as a human being will increase proportionately.

9. Would the world be better or worse if you were never born?

No man is an island; that is to say, "no one can live in this world alone." We all need the help of someone and we can't help coming into contact with and invariably affecting others in some way. The result of our interaction may be as slight as giving or receiving a smile or not that makes us feel better as we walk down the street. It may be as significant as being in the right place to save someone's life.

To have an effect on someone, or be a role model does not always call for a conscious decision. When basketball player Charles Barkley said he is not responsible for raising someone else's child, he was right. On the other hand though, thousands of youngsters and teens do look up to him. Whether it is right is a moot point, the point is that young people do look up to him. He can make a decision to show them that Black men can be good, or he can show them that Black men are bad, but his actions will show whether he consciously decides to do it or not. The irony is that if Mr. Barkley doesn't want to be a role model, but when he tells youngsters to look up to their parents or other positive Black men and women as role models he is being a role model, and not a bad one at that.

10. Would a White supremacist have to lie in order to justify hating you?

The main theme of this book is:

"Black people stand up and be acceptable and respectable." At the same time, White people reject the racists among your number and accept the goodness that you find in Black people. Too many of us are being exactly what we, ourselves should reject. The truth is the truth regardless of who speaks it. The truth is that it is distasteful to be the kind of person that too many of us (Black people) are. As Malcolm X said, "We cannot expect to be accepted by others until we first prove ourselves acceptable."

There are certain justifications for racism directed against people of color in America and the world. Not that racism is justified, but we have to "hang our stupidity" on something:

1. Appearance

Unlike stereotyping, appearance deals with the way a person actually looks, versus the mental exaggeration of what that person is like. The appearance is the attire, facial expression, and gestures.

When a person presents himself or herself to the public, he or she has a certain appearance. If Black youth dressed more conservatively rather than in a Gangsta style, should they not expect to be received accordingly? This is not based on stereotypes as much as awareness that gang members do dress a certain way. There are of course, exceptions to the rule, but I am referring of the norm, not the exception. Though everyone has a right to dress and carry him or herself the way they want to, there are obvious limitations. Just as a waiter can't go to work in a restaurant wearing muscle shirts and sandals, neither can one perform the role of life guard dressed in a three-piece suit and dress shoes. It goes without saying that a person will also dress appropriately for a job interview. It is therefore obvious that the best way to be seen in a better light is to present ourselves as such.

2. Bitterness

The Hatfields and the McCoys were two fictional backwoods families that had been feuding so long that neither side could recall what the original argument was about. There are some people that have been bitter for so long, that like those families they too, don't remember the origin of the anger. When you have that kind of hatred inside you, it must be vented or you will destroy yourself. The easiest targets for White people are nonwhite people. Just as the easiest target for a Black person is a White person. If one lets go of the anger, one will be far less likely exhibit racist behavior.

3. Crime

Primarily because of propaganda, Blacks are expected to be criminal minded. The glorifying of violence, and disrespect for self and others by Rappers does not help expel this negative image. Yes glorifying, because the shooting, banging, fornication, and blatant disrespect for women is not condemned in the music, it is accepted and praised, and therefore glorified. Like the young Malcolm Little (X), if all that we saw of White people was negative, we would also think negatively of them. So we should not expect White people to react any differently if they see enough negative traits in Black people. In this case, knowledge of each other may prove beneficial in stopping racism. It is because of what I know about other races that make it easy for me to accept them. Even if I meet some people that are knuckleheads, I can't judge the whole class as knuckleheads without investigation.

4. Education Level

"Knowledge is power, and power many times corrupts," was the basis of a point made by Minister Louis Farrakhan. He expounded on his belief that when a people with knowledge are entrusted to be in a position over others with lesser knowledge, the party with the greater knowledge has the inherent responsibility of doing what is right by the lesser people. If they instead abuse their position of superiority God Himself, must intervene on behalf of the oppressed people.

5. Ignorance

I am married to a wonderful (White) woman from Budapest, Hungary, though her mother was originally against it. "Why do you have to marry an American, and a Black one at that?" she asked.

I did not fault her, knowing that her position was based on ignorance of African-Americans and me in particular. If the only thing I knew about (us) African-Americans, was that which I saw on TV, I wouldn't want my daughter to marry a Black man either! My mother-in-law accepted me after she came to know me as a person, rather than a negative image. The stereotype was destroyed when she recognized that I am a decent human being, not Black, White, or brown, just human. She did not deny the truth when confronted with it. This truth in essence "set her free from" the ignorance that would have robbed her of the loving relationship with me and her two granddaughters had she remained closed to reality.

As definite as Jesus words that, the truth shall set you free, are the words of Malcolm X, "If you do not want the truth, you don't even deserve freedom." To deserve something is to be worthy of, or merit receiving it. To merit having, is to earn or simply do what it takes to have it. If the truth is the only thing that can set me free, I can in no way merit freedom if I do not accept truth.

Country singer Garth Brooks sings, "When there's only one race and that's mankind, we shall be free . . . When the last thing we notice is the color of skin, and the first thing we look for is the color within, we shall be free."

It is reassuring that someone with a platform is still echoing the dream such as was done by Dr. King. Unlike Dr. King, Mr. Brooks is in no danger of being killed for his views. On the other hand any Black man that has come to the real knowledge of "self" may awaken and inspire other Black. This man is a threat to the powers that be and must be destroyed.

My mother-in-law certainly wasn't the only person to succumb to racial stereotypes. When I was nineteen and living in Louisiana, I began an intimate relationship with a cute and younger, White girl. Perhaps I was "looking for trouble," but it was only by the grace of God that I didn't find it. Late one evening we stood on the corner talking, when a policeman pulled up in his cruiser.

"Is there a problem?" he asked in that "I am above you" tone of voice.

"No, there ain't no problem!" my then, girlfriend barked at him, angry that he would even ask.

I, of course, was humbly quiet, knowing that it was not she but me, in potential danger of being arrested, beaten, shot, etc. In all fairness to policemen, she was much younger than I was. Perhaps this was the reason he elected to stop alongside us that evening.

Nonwhites or Blacks historically, have always offered love, trust, and respect toward the White people. Essentially everywhere White explorers came in contact with nonwhites; they referred to them as savages. These same savages met the White explorers with open arms of friendship, sharing their culture, and on many occasions, such as in what is now America, saving their lives. What did these White explorers do for and to those nonwhite people? They raped, killed, and enslaved them. They destroyed their homes, villages, way of life, and they did much of it in the name of God! Of course the question must be raised, If Black people were in charge, would they do the same thing that the Whites have done? The answer is, "When we look at ancient world history Black people were in charge long before White people came out of the caves of Europe." Recall that the learning institute of the world was at Timbuktu, Africa. Understand that the disciplines such as astronomy, music, art, literature, and architecture of days before Europe began to flourish were common to the Black people of Africa. Archeological finds have proven that Africans came to North and South America long before Columbus. I wholly Malcolm's assertion, "Of all our studies, history is the best qualified to reward our research." With a look at former ages, we learn that not only were Black people of the world in charge, but we were more civilized in the ancient times than some people today.

It is not the Black people that must be taught to love the White people, for we have collectively, always reached out the open hand of brotherhood and peace. It is the White people who must be taught to love the Black people. Proof of our love is the sacrifices made by great, Black men such as Jesus, Gandhi, Martin Luther King, Jr., Medgar Eavers, etc. Let us not forget the forgiveness of Geronimo, Sitting Bull, and thousands of Native Americans who "sat down at the table of brotherhood," only to find plates as empty as the American government's promises. For all his greatness, Dr. King Jr. focused his teachings in the wrong direction. White people should have been taught to turn the other cheek, to love their neighbor, and to honor the words of the Bible, The Constitution of the United States, and the laws of the land!

If you are not convinced, remember that former Klansman, David Duke was forgiven, accepted, and even elected to the Louisiana House of Representatives in 1989, after receiving a notable percentage of Black votes. What has he done in return? He has publicly called for the establishment of civil rights groups for White people! The same thing he did as an active Klansman! Once an advocate of Nazism, Duke said his previous activities had been youthful indiscretions, but even in his campaign he called for equal rights for white people, a Ku Klux Klan hallmark. David Duke and Patrick Buchanan said that they would challenge Pres. George Bush in presidential primary elections in 1992. Duke, a Louisiana state representative, announced his candidacy, Dec. 4. Duke, a former Grand Wizard of the Ku Klux Klan, had just lost a hard-fought campaign for governor of Louisiana, but even in defeat he apparently had attracted a nationwide following.

For a former Grand Wizard of the Ku Klux Klan to garner enough national following to almost bid for the President of the United States, speaks volumes about the state of race relations in America. In the end, he only received about nine percent of the votes for the nomination of his party. Like the plethora of White politicians before him, he has taken forgiveness from Black people and "thrown it into our faces." At the National Press Club, Mr. Duke said, European-Americans face a situation where were going to be outnumbered and outvoted in our own country. Now that's nerve, afraid of being outvoted in the country they stole from the Black people, the Native Americans who forgave and accepted them! Caucasian people whose spread into North America and South America began only a few centuries ago!

Duke further continued that Whites are often refugees in their own communities. Here he implies that the communities are not for all Americans. Nonwhite persons are "outsiders" who in turn make the Whites refugees. Of course this should be no surprise to those who have watched as Duke formed the National Association for the Advancement of White People, leaving that organization only upon being elected to the Louisiana House of Representatives in 1989. The coup de grace is when Duke brings up genocide of White people based on the loss of them as an entity because of present immigration rates. I am sure that Native Americans would have preferred genocide in the form of numbers or interracial marriages versus the loss of human lives they suffered.

6. Inferiority Complex

This one falls squarely into the lap of Black people. Yes, it is true that we have been trained to believe ourselves inferior to White people, but there is more than enough truth to disprove this fallacy. The undeniable truth is that no one man is superior to another simply because of the pigment of his skin. Larry Bird can play basketball far better than I could ever hope to. That doesn't mean I should not strive to be the best that I can be at the sport, or anything I do.

The reason we, as Black people are responsible for our own inferiority complex is, there is no reason to believe such myths as our inferiority to Whites based on racially motivated pseudo investigations. We now know that the American Medical Association was incorrect in stating physical characteristics of Black people was evidence of our inferiority to Whites. We know that the color of skin has nothing to do with our IQ, contrary to Thomas Jefferson's advancement that, "the Blacks are inferior to Whites in both body and mind." A German fellow by the name Adolph Hitler would learn firsthand just how untrue White superiority is, a la track legend Mr. Jessie Owens.

We have just as much access to libraries as anyone. Even if we receive inferior schooling, we can make up the difference in self-study. It is reported though, that only a mere 3 percent of all Americans own library cards. I shudder to think, how many of that three percent are nonwhite. During the period of recognized slavery, it was against the law for slaves to learn how to read and write. This law was established because when a person can read, he again has access to truth that can make him free. Imagine a slave reading the words of famous slave owners and American revolutionaries who wrote and spoke so passionately about the necessity of freedom. A man can see the world very clearly through written words, which have the potential to transform him into living, human potential that does not accept servitude. The man who has an expanding mind cannot long, be bound by any chains. Once the mind is free the body must surely follow; truth will be uncovered sooner or later. Many of the lies told to slaves would have been easily exposed through reading. If slaves read the Bible for themselves, they could see the false religion given to them by the master contradicted the words of The Bible that the master claimed to follow. The Bible also states at Hosea 4:6, Amy people are destroyed for lack of knowledge. If God knows how important knowledge is, we should take that guidance. By the same token, God also commands Christians to abstain from all appearance of evil. Imagine how much better the world would be if we obeyed that command.

The true history of the Black man's arrival in America is written but if we don't read we will never learn that true history. As a person gains knowledge, he has the potential to gain power to direct his or her own destiny. Imagine a slave reading the Constitution stating that all men have the right from God that no one can take away, of life, freedom, and the pursuit of happiness.

Truly, that Klansman spoke correctly when he said, "If you want to keep something away from niggers, write it in a book, because they don't read." Think about it, we have a whole science named after Black people, Egyptology. Yet most Black people don't have a clue that the majority of the people in the Bible were Black. The original Jews were Black, as were Egyptians, the great kings, scientists, and the learned men of antiquity. In fact, much of the greatness of Greece and Rome was plagiarized from Africans. Another example of what we miss because we don't read, though many would say racism is not like it used to be, or nonexistent, you can read in the United States Army manual on Equal Opportunity just how real it is. One can read about Allport's Hierarchy of acting out prejudice. Think about the audacity to even name, define, and spell out prejudice! Allport's Hierarchy consists of Antilocution (disparaging comments and names), Avoidance, Discriminations, Physical Attack, and Extermination. How many times have we suffered the effects of Allport's Hierarchy and not even know that it was so methodical, and admitted in books? I have experienced it in the US Army so that they write about it doesn't mean they don't practice doing it. Of course if Black people read, Whites probably wouldn't write as much about it.

To my knowledge, those who wanted me silenced did not try to kill me, but they certainly made a good attempt destroying my character and disturbing my family. They did attempt to stop my speaking in the same ways that they have always used to stop bold Black men from spreading the truth with conviction. They take your words out of context to make you seem like someone you aren't. They then use that new image to "coerce" you into silence based on your not wanting it to "get out" that you are this new image which they have painted. When this fails, they threaten you with physical violence, or loss of income, prestige, etc. The next step is the physical attack, in my case the end was the loss of income. Fortunately I was moved to a new Duty Station in the Republic of South Korea before I could fall victim to n "accident." So much for the right to free speech. They would not have to exterminate me if they could stop me from speaking to the masses, possibly motivating them. Possibly convincing them to no longer be niggers. I was given a written Counseling Statement by my (racist) Commander. In the statement he informed me that I was "not to talk about politics, history, or religion." To this I informed him that if he had the authority to give me such a command, he might as well chapter me out of the Army because it (spreading the Christian Gospel) was the reason that I came into the Army.

Now, that we can't blame others for how we feel about ourselves, what happens if when we no longer have an inferiority complex? I was sent to a psychiatrist because of memory problems and headaches. In the process of treatment I told my White doctor that I believed at regular intervals in history; a great leader arises among the people to change the world. I expressed my belief that I could very well be that man for our time. He wrote in my evaluation that I had Delusions of Grandeur. You could, if you knew your history, rattle off the names of White men who proclaimed the desire to be so great that they would change the world. Does anyone say Alexander the Great, Napoleon Bonaparte, George Washington, or Christopher Columbus had Delusions of Grandeur? Is it a delusion that great Black men built the pyramids that even today, with all our technology, cannot be reproduced? Was it a delusion that gave the Black men of old the ability to chart the skies? If greatness in Black people is a delusion, what are we to say about the great Black people who did change, or help change the world: Jesus, Moses, Crispus Attucks, Mahatma Gandhi, Martin Luther King, Jr., Malcolm X, and etcetera?

7. Social Status

If we are aware that a class of people is below us in terms of education, finances, or social status, is your attitude toward them positive or negative? Are we to hate them? More likely than not, if those persons are beneath us in social status, the tendency is to reason that these people are also beneath us mentally, and morally. Of course, there are exceptions to almost every rule, but this mentality tends to hold true. People tend to believe that the things you have make you a better than others who have less. Is it any wonder it is said,"The clothes make the man?" If we don't have many material possessions, rather than lift ourselves up, do we merely find someone to be seen as beneath us? When we realize that we are this or that regardless of our possessions, we will have made another step on our way to making the world a better place.

The flip side of the coin is the subconscious belief that because we don't have much, we are subordinate to those who do have much.

This is especially true when we have little in the way of material goods. As long as this mind is in us, and we don't have much, they will feel subordinate to those who do. If we believe we are inferior, then we act in an inferior manner, thus becoming inferior. The scripture rings true, "As a man thinketh, so is he." The supremacy of the White person over the Black seems evident partly because the Black man debases himself. When Blacks refuse the educated tongue because it sounds like you are trying to be White, reject desk jobs for macho, menial labor, he makes himself inferior.

When a person feels inferior to someone, many times he compensates for it by finding someone he can see as beneath himself. Well-to-do Whites for instance, see poor Whites as poor White trash, who then place Black people beneath White trash in the pecking order of life. The thinking should be, "I am going to strive to better myself and the world, without regard to what others wrongly think of me. No matter what material things I have or have not and especially despite what anyone says I can't do."

8. Stereotyping

Stereotyping, as wrong as it may be, does not always originate with the person holding untrue beliefs about others. Too many times they'll show young, Black, men attempt to prove their Blackness, by acting out certain stereotypes about themselves! Brothers play the dozens, pretending to be down, and are rarely, if ever are into books, knowledge, and learning. They know that just because someone looks like a thug, doesn't mean they actually are criminals, but police officers that are constantly arresting actual criminals that fit the description cannot be blamed for at least some profiling. Should they not be wary of someone that looks like what appears to be the majority of criminals? It would be unwise on their part to not be wary.

Yes, you do have the right to dress, act, and talk in the manner you choose. So too did the scores of innocent Black men, arrested because they fit the profile! "Are you willing to risk your freedom, and possibly your life, just to look down, hip, or cool?"

Regardless of how one may feel about it, or whether they choose to admit it or not, it does matter a great deal what other people think of you. (See chapter 10). Before people can demand respect, they must be deserving of that respect. If a man does not deserve respect, others may mimic respect for him out of fear, embarrassment, etc. In the US Army for example, soldiers are commanded to respect a person's rank and position, regardless of the personal character of the person holding that rank, position, or title. Soldiers are commanded to salute a vehicle that has the insignia of an officer. The command is not to salute the person in the vehicle, but the vehicle itself! This emphasizes that respect is afforded to that which is deserving of respect, the position. Those in positions that warrant respect should carry themselves in a manner, which warrants our respect the person, but that is not always the case. It is possible for someone as young as 23 years old to enter the Army as a Second Lieutenant. With as little as six months in the Army that Lieutenant outranks a First Sergeant who has been in the Army longer than that Lieutenant has been alive! The First Sergeant must refer to that young Lieutenant as "sir," snap to attention, and render a hand salute as a show of respect. That First Sergeant goes through the motions, but who honestly believes a forty-year-old First Sergeant with more than twenty years in the Army actually respects a twenty-three-year-old Lieutenant with as little as six months' time in the service?

9. Superiority Complex

"We hold these truths to be self-evident, that all men are created equal . . ."

Words are very powerful when spoken or heard by someone who believes them. Unfortunately, the writer of the above words neither meant them, nor spoke them to persons who believed them. We know that some of the founding fathers owned slaves, and considered nonwhites worth only a fraction of the worth of Whites. Once again, though, I ask that we be honest. Are all men created equally? If not, how are men created differently, if so, where do we begin to excel past another? Are any two babies born with the same health, the same safe and loving environment? Are any two babies kept safe and nurtured from their parents, in the same manner? Lastly, do even Siamese twins grow to be the same in adulthood? Of course not, but they can share the same potential. The person that acts on his own potential, setting realistic goals and never giving up will be guaranteed success.

In the Diary of Anne Frank, we read, [Daddy] said, "All children must look after their own upbringing. Parents can only give good advice or put them on the right paths, but the final forming of a person's character lies in their own hands."

The infamous slave owner William Lynch said to slave owners in South Carolina that they could put a nigger in a pig pen and he will accept it with no complaint but to ask you for cleaning supplies if he bothers you at all or bothers to clean it. All you have to do is use the right words. On the other hand, if you use the wrong wording, you will find that same nigger trying to get into your house. "Why do we stay in the Federal Housing Projects and do not aspire to greatness?" "Have we been told so long that niggers can't so we don't?" Project; consider the words that are synonymous with project: scheme, plan, mission, and undertaking. Housing scheme, housing plan, housing mission, housing undertaking. I use my own money to "house" roaches in "Roach Motels" because I don't want the undesirables living alongside me. Yes, it is a scheme, plan, mission, or undertaking that I have used my own resources on for the greater comfort I receive by segregating them from my family and myself.

10. Tradition

It is a powerful inquiry to ask, "Why do you believe what you believe, follow what you follow, belong to what you belong to?"

"That's the way I was raised. That's the way it has always been. That's the way my parents taught me," are some of the answers given, but only means, "That's what my parents believed, so I believe it too."

Should we blindly accept what we are told without question, simply because it came from an authority figure? Consider the beliefs of the founding fathers in regard to nonwhite persons, our nineteen sixties government in regard to racial equality, the public school systems false history of mankind, the many false religious leaders, and people that are held in high esteem. Now consider the words of Sir Francis Bacon: Do not accept any situation, question, argue and explore.

God Himself commands at Malachi 3:10 of the Bible, "Prove me." In the New Testament He speaks through the apostle Paul at I Thessalonians 5:21 that Christians are to "prove all things, (and) hold fast that which is good." Based on what the world today calls Christianity, people have ceased proving anything, and are strongly holding to that which is unarguably not truth! Tradition for the sake of tradition is proven unwise when consider such things as racism, and even soul food. Boys and girls grow up hating people because their parents gave them the ridiculous notion of hating people because of the color, merely because their parents did. Soul food us merely a nice way of say slave food. It was not our great, great, grandparents desire to eat pig intestines, and hogs heads. Then the addition of spices and seasonings, was only to make the naturally repugnant rations palatable

11. Subconscious Heredity?

Why is their racism in America? What is the origin of past life regression? Do these two themes have anything in common? The two themes have in common that the mind must regurgitate something so deep in its own subconscious that it many times will only manifest itself accidentally.

Envision this scenario: After a car accident a woman experiences memories of being a child in eighteenth century England. On the other hand a White guy with Black friends slips when he gets drunk and a Black steps on his expensive, new shoes. Does he in anger call him nigger?

In past life regression (memories of a time long before you were born), my theory is that just as a child inherit its father or mothers eyes, hair, etc., it may be possible that juices found in the brain of the parent or parents are passed through the umbilical cord. Memories, thoughts, dream, and ideas though, in a sense real and yet intangible travel inside very tangible brains. Perhaps a small portion of the parent's memory is passed on from parent to child. Then again when that child becomes a parent, the memory is passed on down several succeeding generations as body fluids are exchanged in the sexual consummation of each succeeding marriage. The memory may not be activated for several generations as it is passed down the line. So what memory do some White people hold that makes them react so hatefully toward Black people? What memories do Black people hold that makes us so quick to forgive them? Why is it so easy for a few White people to take over a whole country? We know at least one thought pattern that is not a memory but very powerful in misguiding the psyche of Black people, specifically African-Americans. The idea that Black people were living at a sub human level in Africa, and were made better off in America, even as slaves. Because of the popular belief that anything America allows minorities to have is better than what they had prior to slavery, it is easy to accept poverty, ignorance, and handouts that eventually "make the benefactor the jailer." When you accept a gift from someone, they invariably, want something in return. Whether it's the feeling that comes with doing a good deed, blessings from a higher power, a favor in return, or something far less noble, there has to be payment for all we get from others. If I were to give you a thousand dollars a month and not require you to work for it or pay it back, wouldn't you wonder what I expected in return? What do politicians get in return for sustaining welfare as a way of life for generations? It seems to be used as a tool to promote racism justified by the belief that the majority of people on Welfare are Black, or is it to keep minorities and poor White people from realizing their potential as human beings via Capitalism?

Considering the fact that there is a finite amount of money in circulation, if everyone strove to be financially independent, the money would spread thin and the riches of the rich would not be as rich. This is a possible reason for the continued acceptance of a Welfare system in America. Could it be that the government is more willing to give away (invest) a few hundred dollars into single parent families hoping to sustain the "Welfare cycle?" Why is it illegal for an insurance salesman to offer his products and services to a person on Welfare? I know this to be true in California, so how many other states have the same law? Is it that the potential to break the Welfare cycle upon receipt of a sizable sum of money might enable the child of a deceased Welfare parent to pay for school or start a small business, that may lead to success or financial freedom? Even a fool could get a foothold on the American Dream with enough capital, just as even a slave could gain self-esteem and freedom with the applied wisdom found in books. As Brother Malcolm said, "This country is so diabolical, that it has the seeds of its own destruction right in it."

Have you ever considered the economic repercussions caused by the abolition of slavery? Imagine the upheaval to a strong business utilizing of free labor if it suddenly had to pay its thousands of employees even a onetime settlement? This is the reason America can't make restitution to the descendants of slaves. Knowing this, would it not be noble of her to encourage those same descendants to do for them to be financially free. The words of Malcolm X again ring true, "When you have to depend on your enemy for food, you are in bad shape."

Enemy-1. A person who hates another, and wishes or tries to hurt him; foe. 2. A person hostile to an idea, cause, etc. 3. Anything injurious or harmful. It is clear whom our enemies are when we consider a person's standing in relation to our own well being. If racism was only a matter of hating you because you hate me, then the only thing necessary to stop racism would before love, at which point there would be no reason for racism. If you hate me simply because I hate you, you should then love me if I love you? This experiment was tried, and Doctor Martin Luther King Jr. lost his life, as did Jesus of Nazareth, proving that there are those who will hate you no matter how much you love them.

CHAPTER FIVE

Father Have You Forsaken Us?

There are two categories of Jews; there are the original Jews who are direct blood descendants of the Hebrew patriarch Abraham, and they are not Caucasian. The others are the Caucasian, proselyte or converted Jews, such as those who suffered during the German Holocaust.

According to Microsoft Encarta 98 Encyclopedia, during the first half of the 20th century, and particularly in the period between World War I and World War II, anti-Semitism became a dominant force in European politics, notably in Germany. In the 1930s the growth of National Socialism, incorporating anti-Semitic doctrines, threatened all <u>Jews, many of who considered themselves not Jews but assimilated members of various national groups</u>.

During the supremacy of the National Socialists in Western Europe, an estimated 6 million European-Jews were slaughtered, both in Germany and in German-controlled states. This period of persecution and extermination of European-Jews is called the

Holocaust. The proselyte Jew is Jewish by religion, having been converted to Judaism. Just as the White Jesus slowly overtook the image of the real Jesus, the White Jews have taken the place of the original Jews. Like the cup of coffee Malcolm X spoke of which has had so much cream added that it no longer looks like coffee. The original Jews are brothers in color to the African and African-American. That, which is shared by us, connects us.

The scriptures of the Bible seem to point to African-Americans when God admonishes the Jewish people, at Deuteronomy 11:27-28 that as long as they obeyed Him, they could not lose, but if they chose to be disobedient, they would be utterly destroyed. Hebrews chapter 12 explains the purpose of chastisement including the fact that a son is not truly a son if he is not chastised. In fact it reads that a disobedient son is not love or truly a son if his parents do not chastise him. Because of our sojourn as slaves and utter destruction as a people, we seem to have received that chastisement. Whether this punishment was meant for the Black manof America is questionable, but who but the African-American can say they have been utterly destroyed? Don't think that just because we still exist, we are not destroyed! If you don't think we're destroyed, tell me your last name and speak to me in your original language. Webster's New World Dictionary defines destroy as to tear down; demolish, to spoil completely; ruin, to put to an end, to kill, "to neutralize the effect of, and to make useless." "Now tell me we haven't been destroyed! Tell me there are no more niggers! When we wake up and stand up, then we will no longer be niggers. It won't be up to others to tell us we're accepted when we become acceptable to ourselves!"

The truth can be found in tracing the Black man of America directly to the continent of Africa. It is there that we may or may not be traced to the children of Israel. The challenge is to know with certainty, but even if Deuteronomy 11:27-28 is not directed at specifically and only to all nonwhite persons, it still remains applicable today. People of color around the world could lay claim to this chastisement, because of the history of destruction in our differing cultures. In my admittedly, limited study of the German Holocaust, I have come to lean strongly toward the possibility that the proselyte Jews of Nazi Germany were destroyed because they, as White people, chose to assimilate into a Black religion, Judaism! I believe this is the missing factor in the history of the Holocaust. I have not come across a more clear answer for the cause of Adolph Hitler's hatred and willingness to exterminate the Caucasian Jewish people of Germany. For Hitler, a White supremacist, seeing Whites accept a historically nonwhite religion was akin to a member of the Nation of Islam observing Blacks accepting what they consider as the White religion, of Christianity. The irony being that true Christianity is of a nonwhite origin. True Christianity does not judge people on the basis of skin color. The Religion that Minister Louis Farrakhan and other ministers of the NOI speak out against is not true Christianity. The (so-called) Christian Knights of the Ku Klux Klan are <u>not</u> and never were Christians! The myriad of denominations (divisions) of what was originally singular and true Christianity, have clouded the truth and caused many people to reject God because of evil deeds men have done in the name of God. I can't help but wonder what would have become of Malcolm Little if he had met some true Christians during his formative years. Would he have ever become a "Black Muslim" or later, converted further to Orthodox Islam?

In the Book of Revelations, of the Holy Bible, chapter 12, you can read about "a woman clothed with the sun, pregnant with a man-child," a son. There appears a great red dragon, the Devil that wants to kill her man-child. When God protects the woman and her child, the Devil is angered and goes on to make war with the descendants of the son whom he could not kill. Neither the woman, the son, nor the descendants of the man-child were forsaken of God. As if in fulfillment of that prophecy, our forefathers were killed and many were brought to this country as slaves. Slaves in America were not seen as human beings, but White America was willing to put up with them as long as it benefited the slave owners. After their complete emancipation, Black people were hated with a greater passion. When we were no longer of benefit to them (racist Whites), they no longer wanted us around. Who do you suppose was told, "go west?" I say "we," because Black people today cannot be detached from our past. If we do not have some link to the men and women that lived and died, in the process of making America, then we forfeit our claim on America. We are citizens not because of the benevolence of, White America, but because we have earned that right. We are heirs to America, which is why we say "we," when we talk about our forefathers. When White people speak of the founding fathers, and the pilgrims, they say "we," though they like us, weren't there. Being descendants of the "man-child" stolen from Africa. I say stolen rather than kidnapped, because we weren't considered humans that we could be kidnapped, but soul-less property, that could be stolen.

I could not say that the Black man in America is actually the fulfillment of that specific prophecy but I can say the many times the spiritual is reflected in the physical. Much like the Bible account, we see that a dragon as racism which is still waging war against the descendants of the slaves. As the Devil tried to destroy Gods plan of salvation for mankind, by destroying the man-child. In a like manner, there seems to have been a scheme afoot to destroy Blacks and their descendants. The Tuskegee tests (if you call injecting men with Venereal Disease testing) that were done on Black men, the distribution of birth control pills, the pumping of alcohol and drugs into the Black communities.

What do the heterosexual Black men in Africa and the homosexual White men in America have in common? Here's a hint to AIDS; keep in mind that Hitler's mentality, as a White supremacist. The white supremacist chooses to ignore, debunk, or destroy those whom they view as less than "superior" Whites. Let us never forget The Trail of Tears, Wounded Knee, or the countless campaigns of genocide directed against Native Americans.

Jesus said at Matthew 6:33, "Seek ye first the kingdom of God and His righteousness and all these things will be added unto you." God promises that if we obey Him, we will be successful. Today many Black men and women are striving to unite Black communities, but there will be no real unity until we come back to God. Today Black people throughout the world and certainly throughout America live not forsaken of God, but forsaking God!

CHAPTER SIX

To Make A Slave

Minister Farrakhan made an outstanding point about slavery. In paraphrase: If God has the power to allow or stop anything He chooses, why would he allow us to go through slavery? He, Minister Farrakhan, put forth that there must be a lesson we were to learn. I say we weren't supposed to learn from our experience, it was because of what we as a people had been guilty of, that God chose to chastise us. We know that disobedience to God leads to chastisement, what He desires is that our chastisement leads to repentance. When my mother used a leather belt to chastise me, I did not then begin to hate all leather belts. The slavers were only the tools God used to chastise, and His chastisement was meant to bring the disobedient back to obedience. God Himself declares at Hebrews 12:6, "For those whom I loveth, I chasteneth." The question is, will we accept Gods chastisement and repent, or will we now hate all White people and die in our sins?

Black people generally are not well versed on how to <u>properly</u> forgive. The proper way to forgive is to release any animosity and let God pass judgment and chastise if need be. Before one can forgive though, forgiveness must be requested. We tend to hold resentment because we do not see the justice of our being wronged. For the unrepentant, and the sincere request of forgiveness we do not see justice because the system is on the side of the antagonist. Spiritual justice that is meted out by God against the oppressors and enemies of His people, goes unfulfilled because many of us know that God is not on our side. God is only with the righteous, the obedient, and those who are honestly following His will to the absolute best of their ability. If there is no chastisement, the wrong stays with us, we can't honestly forgive because our enemies have asked for it, or offered restitution for the error of their ways. "Vengeance is mine sayeth the Lord," Romans 12:19-21. According to the Bible at Luke 12:10, James 5:15, I John 5:16, even God does not forgive unless we first ask.

CHAPTER SEVEN

Foxes and Wolves

"The Law of Tooth and Fang is kill or be killed; eat or be eaten!" This is a very true saying, literally in the wild animal kingdom, and figuratively in man's world. Sometimes though, it becomes literal for men too. History conveys that no people ever rose up from unfair servitude or slavery to gain freedom without the shedding of blood. Our own American Revolution typifies the idea of revolution being violent. Though Mahatma Gandhi's non-violent revolution may be sighted along with that of the late Dr. Martin Luther King Jr. as examples of revolution without bloodshed, this is not so. Thousands of human lives were lost as men determined to not render evil for evil against their attackers and accusers, spilled their own blood. Gandhi is quoted to have said, "If I had the choice between being thought coward and violence, I would choose violence."

Dr. King did not live to see the movement into its logical role of self-defense, but it seems that civil rights were mainly achieved because of the nonwhite people's refusal to accept the Anon scriptural turn the other cheek doctrine. Yes, non-scriptural. Jesus words to his disciples to turn the other cheek were not a call to martyrdom, but a guide to not seek vengeance beyond understandable self-defense. Jesus cry was to "not render railing for railing." His was not the call to let the lions have their way. Evidence to this is Jesus refusal to let Himself be thrown off the side of a hill and killed at the beginning of His ministry, as detailed at Luke 4:28-30. When He did give His life, He gave it; not in the spirit of pacifism, but as a sacrifice with the ability to choose sacrifice. Only in obedience to his heavenly father's will that he be a sacrifice for man's sins did he offer up His life, but only when it was time for that sacrifice! If I were a betting man, I would bet that the moneychangers in the temple did not think of Jesus as a pacifist!

Canines have been the perpetrators of White supremacy even until this day. When (White racist) men act out in animalistic ways towards their fellow (Black pacifist) man we akin them to wolves and the pacifist as sheep. When the wolves try to hide their evil belief system, they are characteristic of foxes. The presence of wolves among Americans was evident in the 60's, but the belief system that spawned them is not dissolved today. Today the wolf has become the fox, smiling before the world, but hiding a heart that is fully evil.

Investigative news programs have broadcast stories showing the differences in the treatment of Whites versus the treatment of Blacks. When two people with hidden cameras spend a week doing everyday things, we as people need to do; viewers can see the deep-seated racial bias in white business owners and apartment managers for example. Time after time we see the White person being greeted with open arms (sometimes literally) at stores, car dealerships, and apartment complexes. When the Black person approaches the same businesses he or she is sometimes completely ignored. He is told there are no more vacancies, or job positions available and even tailed in department stores! When the news program confront those establishments about their practices, they claim immediately that they do not practice any bias towards their customers, that they treat everyone the same, they try to fox their way out of the obvious show of racism. These are the things we would have expected to happen in 1960, we would be surprised if it did not occur then. Today though, in the year two thousand, men still can't treat each other with dignity simply because of the color of their skin!

In 1996 my then wife, and I went to purchase a new car. We decided on a Jeep Cherokee, but after producing the required proof of income, identity, etc., I still did not qualify for the automobile. I came up with the "brilliant" suggestion that we try to get the car in my wife's name alone. My wife filled out paperwork and was approved to buy the car in her name only. My wife was not required to show the proofs that I had been required to produce. This White woman who was not yet an American citizen, whose only source of income was the pay for working for my small publishing company! Then there was my Army Company Commander whom I had gone to about the racist remark of a White soldier. In his anger my Company Commander admitted to me that he has "racist feelings," but is "trying to work through them!" As if that were not bad enough, when I reported it to my Battalion Commander, his reply was, "Well at least he's being honest.

I don't know why, but my chain of command decided to send me to an Equal Opportunity Training Course. Perhaps they thought I would learn something that would make me think the overabundance of racism did not exist at Fort Carson. I learned a lot including the fact that a female Military Policeman in that class had been hearing "some type of racist or sexist remark at least once a week!" There lies an argument against women in combat: The White policewoman was confronted with an enemy and she "didn't have a clue" what should be done, she just "let it slide!" She gave justification to my beliefs about policemen, while at the same time she did not take a stand against the remarks either. If you are not Black, you probably don't consider how far we have <u>not</u> come in regards to Civil Rights, Human rights, or common decency. On one occasion, I was taken in by a con man. Probably because of my strong desire to help others, I believed this con artist and for it I was punished (without an <u>honest</u> investigation) for mail. It didn't matter that the Military Criminal Investigators, the civilian criminal investigators, the Denver Supreme Court accepted the facts that I was innocent of any intentional wrongdoing or criminal intent. Unfortunately my judge and jury in a Field Grade Article 15 proceeding (military version of a trial), just happened to be my Battalion Commander and admittedly racist Company Commander! The military criminal investigator, who investigated my case, spoke on my behalf, then to add insult to injury, my civilian lawyer did not show up, nor did he to subpoena the civilian investigator who would have spoken in my defense. As Malcolm X pointed out, "When you look to your enemy for justice, you never get any." For me there was no justice, "just us;" my 'lynchers,' and myself.

Lastly, I was talking to a White soldier who was considered a "wanna be" (Black), by his White peers. I say peers because they don't consider him a friend of theirs. He dresses, acts, and talks like a Black person, listening to Black music, and they reject him for it. This soldier who is rejected by his fellow White soldiers, confessed to me that he would "take the side of a White person who is wrong over a Black person who is right!"

For the nonwhite reader, I am sure you need no examples of racism in America, I am confident you have personally experienced it. You see the overt racism, the wolves. On the other hand if you are White, you may find my words hard to accept. I understand that, since you have not been a victim of racism all the days of your life. There are Whites who, though they are not racist, have experienced reverse racism. As stated earlier though, because nonwhites generally do not have the power to act out their reverse racist feeling, Whites only suffer occasional name calling or a fist fight at worst. This is the extent of Allport's Hierarchy of Acting Out Prejudice. I may have to give you some other examples of open racism I have been a victim to such as being fired from a job after my boss learned that my wife was White. Being referred to as "nigger" by a shopper at a California Wal Mart. My wife being told there were no more open apartments (though she was about to interview for one) after I came in from parking the car. If you do not believe me, ask any Black person if they have experienced any type of overt or covert racism. See how many you will meet that can give testimony from their own life, before you meet one that cannot.

CHAPTER EIGHT

Self-Hate vs. Self-Love

There are literally, hundreds of books on the subject of self-esteem (self-love) and the effect it has on people. There is one book that I know of which accurately defines love: The Holy Bible. There is a definition of love in the dictionaries, but what truly is love?

Love is not simply a feeling, as defined in the dictionary. I say that substantive love is sacrifice, and commitment! If I love you, I am willing to sacrifice for you, I am committed to you, and I desire only the best for you. If I love you I do not need specific commandments of what to do and what not to do towards you. This is why Jesus said, "All the law (Ten Commandments) is fulfilled in one word: love." Not just love but that we would love each other enough to lay down our life for another!

Directly linked to self-love is the tenet of "loving your neighbor as yourself." Minister Farrakhan explained that "Love of neighbor is predicated upon love of self. That one cannot love another until he loves himself is clearly misinterpretation of scripture since judging by our treatment of and attitude toward each other. While we have proven to be hateful, to the point of murdering each other, we still love the White people of the world to the point of reverence, seeing them as intellectually superior to us. I have to disagree with Minister Farrakhan, understanding that Jesus point was not that one must love himself first, but that most men do love themselves and want what is best for themselves. Therefore, we should treat our neighbors with that high degree of love and respect. Today it seems the number of men who do not love themselves outnumber the number of men who do love themselves. I am not referring to narcissism, Imp referring to the desire to have, be, and do what is right for, and in one's own best interest. If men did not hate themselves, there would be no drug addiction, crime, hatred, or any of the other destructive vices that hinder us as a people.

If I love myself, I am happy with myself (and those who look like me). I will not seek to do nothing evil against those whom I am happy with. When we are happy with our brothers and sisters in color, the natural compulsion is to Ado good to them. Love of self and love of fellow man becomes a self-affecting cycle and our self-esteem grows proportionately causing us to commit to doing, being, and seeking that which is in our best interest? Self-esteem becomes the catalyst for a wide range of changes because I won't need White peoples' acceptance to feel self-worth. I will not degrade myself to be accepted begrudgingly by those who do not want association with me. Notice that if we weren't so determined to be a part of White America, we would have our own businesses, neighborhoods, jobs, and leaders. We don't want all Black institutions because we don't feel we can accomplish the things we need to accomplish alone. We do feel inferior to Whites! If we didn't we would not be working so hard to be a part of his world, we would work just as hard or harder to make our own. I am not saying, "Let's revert back to segregation with its politics of separate and unequal." I am saying accept loving friendship and brotherhood of all those who honestly want brotherhood and friendship but don't force your way into where you are not wanted. We have forced our way into exclusively White organizations such as the Masons, we have forced our way into the military branches, dying for the American way and those who did survive America's wars, did so only to face another war here in America!

You can almost judge a book (person's self-esteem) by its cover (outward appearance) when it comes to the average person. This may not be the appropriate way to view people and/or interact with them, but so much can be deduced about a person merely by evaluating their outer coverings. Outer coverings include clothing, attachments to clothing, hairstyle, makeup, speech, tattoos, hand gestures, etc. Sociologists agree that some examples of symbolic communication are hair, signs, and clothes. People make louder statements about themselves by these measures than by words. So it is critical that we don't send the wrong message because when we want to appear as others, who may mean the message that is being sent.

I am not justifying stereotyping; I am talking about generalizations. Generalizations are acceptable where stereotyping is not because stereotyping is based on exaggerated and untrue beliefs about people. Generalizations are based on what is generally true about people. For instance, one cannot say, all Preachers are only interested in money, but one could say that generally most Preachers are willing to help strangers. Of course there are exceptions to the rule, but in general it is true that most Preachers are willing to help strangers.

If anyone wants to be respected as a human being and not pre-judged or suffer as a stereotype, we must first understand the nature of people to unconsciously pre-judge to some degree. If we see someone in a bank wearing a long trench coat on a hot, dry, summer, day we can't stop the suspicious thoughts that will of course, come to mind. Evaluate yourself and ask, "Is it the spirit of self-love or self-hate that motivates me to do the things I do?"

1. Appearance

If we do not want to be thought of as a trouble making, thug, "gang-banger," they must refrain from the garb that is generally worn by those persons. If we want to be respected and taken seriously, we must present ourselves appropriately. All gang-bangers may not wear baggy pants and beepers, but we must take into consult the fact that many do. We should never give the impression that we are a part of any class that justifies our being hated. Once we are known, at school, work, etc., then we are at liberty to dress a little more uniquely. Is wrong to pierce ones eyebrow, and tongue? It is if you want to be taken serious as a mature adult. Would you feel comfortable if the man that was scheduled to operate on you wore a Mohawk hairdo and several body piercings?

2. Crime

The logical consequence of crime is suffering. The criminal may not be conscious of his own suffering because of the emotional sedation of revenge, anger, excitement, etc. When the booty is captured, you feel you've won that it is only the victim that suffers. Many times the perpetrator is unaware of the increased potential to commit similar or greater crimes. As one performs an action repeatedly, it becomes proportionately easier to perform that action and to a greater degree of severity. The logic is that as the intensity and occurrence increases, the potential to be caught in the act or found out is also magnified. If arrested, the suffering is visible to the criminal, but if the criminal is not apprehended all Blacks suffers. Those who only remotely resemble the actual criminal appear suspect in the eyes the White public. Instead of judging correctly the shortcomings of the criminal that is Black, Blacks as a whole are classified as criminals. This is why Black people cannot afford the spiritual, mental, and morally blind people who happen to be Nonwhite! Too many times, "Justifiable Homicide" is the name of "Death" for the Afro-American male. We become accessories to the crime of police brutality when we justify for them, the idea that Black people are criminals. The infamous "Rodney King beating" is a grave testimony of society's using the Black man's breaking of the law to overshadow the White police officers' own breaking of the law. Regardless of the law or laws broken by Rodney King, what fool could "honestly" say, "The man in the video was a danger to the police officers?" Yet King's antagonists got away with it to a large degree. The resulting riots once again proved that when dealing with Whites, it is the language of violence that they understand, and which leads to results. It worked for them for hundreds of years, now it has worked against them. In the words of Malcolm X, "This is the only language they understand. You cannot come to them with love; they do not understand that. If you come to them with some power and unyielding resolve, then you will get some kind of action from them."

Malcolm pointed out that William Shakespeare penned for the character Hamlet, "To be or not to be, that is the question. Whether it be nobler in the minds of men to suffer the slings and arrows of outrageous misfortune or by taking up arms against a sea of troubles, by opposing them, end them."

It seems that one of the greatest writers of all time believed in the logical human right to self-preservation through justifiable self-defense. Faced with a "sea of troubles," the genius of Dr. Martin Luther King, Jr. believed differently. I would love to have talked to Dr. King, to gain from him the basis of his illogical belief system. I think it is a well-kept secret that the gains in Civil Rights were made primarily, if not solely due to Black peoples taking up arms against a sea of troubles.

When Black people remained passive when attacked, there was no hint of compassion from their attackers or White America as a whole. There was no justice for Blacks even from the most powerful man in America, then, President, John F. Kennedy. I do not advocate violent revolution, but the time for Black people to intellectually rise up and aggressively throw off the shackles of ignorance, poverty, and low self-esteem is now! When we do this we can achieve that end through nonviolent use of the uniting, and educating ourselves beyond the biased, (mis)education offered to us in schools, colleges, and universities throughout America. We have the means of effecting change today without shedding blood.

3. Education Level

"To love education, wisdom, and knowledge is to love self." One can achieve virtually anything if he has the knowledge of "how." One can go anywhere if he has the knowledge of how, and one can learn essentially anything if he simply gets a library card and uses it. I am of course, aware that this is not the only route to self-education. Today we have almost boundless access to information via the Internet, get a library card is a catch phrase synonymous with educate yourself. It is no surprise to those of us who are listening that the current education system is not designed to equip the masses, Black or White, the tools necessary to be successful. If you believe you've been equipped with more than a fancy paper that allows you work for someone else, then explain purpose and origin of the Electoral College, the function of politics, the actual doctrines of Christianity as found in the Bible. Clearly explain the Rule of 72, or the difference between saving and investing.

There are methodical steps to achievement, and each step calls for knowledge. To not seek knowledge is to say; I don't care to better myself. To not care to better your self is to say; I don't care about myself. To not care about yourself, is no different than saying, "I don't love myself." No matter what <u>reasonable</u> goal you want to achieve, if you follow the pattern below and never give up those reasonable dreams and goals you will be able to succeed:

1. Set Reasonable Goal(s)

Set the long-range goal of what you want to achieve in your lifetime. Set short-range goals that as you accomplish them, will lead to achievement your long-range goal.

2. Research Your Goal(s)

Find out what you must do to achieve the goals you have set, and determine if you actually want to do what it takes to achieve your goals.

3. Align Your Goal(s) with Your Values

If the things that are important to you conflict with the things you must do to achieve your goals, the chances are very high that you will not achieve your goals, unless you compromise your values (which make them not valuable).

4. Make Your Goal(s) Tangible

Get a picture of something that depicts your goal in some way, this will bring your goals to the fore and keep you mindful of them. People, who make their goals tangible, are more likely to achieve them than those who merely set goals in their minds.

5. Most Importantly, Put God First

If you are not religious, then you will not apply this element, but I challenge even you to honestly seek the Lord, and know for yourself that He is and He will bless those who submit to Him. He will insure we have all the other things we need in life. I emphasize need versus want since many times we choose the things we want over the things we need. For example, as a single man I need a place to live, but I don't need a five-bedroom mansion (unless I plan to move my family in or some other circumstance that would warrant that much room.

Additional Points:

Research Other Peoples Success

Research what others have done to achieve the same goal you have set for yourself. You don't have to use trial and error, since someone has already done it before you. It is quite possible that you will be able to find the story of successful people at your nearest library. Simply apply the things that they did that worked, this will save you the time, money, and effort of attempting to do something that will not lead to the achievement of your dreams and goals. When you are able to avoid time-consuming mistakes, you will then see the extreme importance of a library card.

Never Abandon Your <u>Reasonable</u> Dream(s) or Goal(s)

Reasonable goals coupled with knowledge and perseverance practically guarantees success. As you achieve your short-range goals they will ultimately lead to the achievement of your long-range goal(s), but if you give up or allow someone to steal your dreams, you are guaranteed failure. As you move towards success, you will probably have set backs, but ultimately failure can only occur when or if you give up.

Establish short-range goals and knowledge coupled with perseverance often invariably leads to success in reaching or achieving those short-range goals. Achieving short-range goals through perseverance likewise almost guarantees successful achievement of long range goals. Consistent achievement of long range goals balanced by the non-material but equally important things in life will lead to a successful life. Note that with perseverance and a realistic goal, success is almost always assured! In reality some unforeseen event can thwart the best-laid plans, but intermediate failure is to be expected along the path to final success in any endeavor. Temporary setbacks are only synonymous with failure when we give up our dreams and goals and accept defeat.

Use the Success Prompter below to chart your path to success:

Short Range Goal(s)	Steps to be Taken	Long Range Goal(s)	Success
1	2	3	4
1	2	3	4
1	2	3	4
1	2	3	4

Directions-Enter the appropriate information that applies you. If you find that there are necessary steps in the achievement of your goals that you do not wish to fulfill, simply enter a new long range goal that includes only the short ranges goals and steps which you are willing to perform in order to achieve your goal(s).

1-List short range goals that upon completion of each will move you closer to your long-range goal.

2-List the actual steps that need to be taken in the achievement of short range goals.

3-List long range goals that will be achieved when all short-range goals are achieved.

4-List the detail what you hope to be the result of your successful achievement of your long-range goal(s).

3.   Ignorance

Ignorance and ignorant are not bad words, although they are commonly used in a negative connotation. Ignorance is simply the lack of knowledge about something. There are enough things that each man is ignorant of, to compose a completely new world! Illiterate, uneducated, unenlightened, unlearned, blind, unaware, uninformed, unknowing, backward, crude, primitive are all-synonymous with the word ignorant. These words describe too many Black people. If we are honest, they may apply to you, the reader, but this is not a shame.

The shame is in seeing that you are ignorant and doing nothing to correct it. Bruce Lee said, "He who knows not, and knows not he knows not is foolish, shun him. He who knows not, and knows he knows not is simple, teach him. He who knows not, and knows not he knows not is asleep, awaken him. He who knows and knows he knows, is wise, follow him."

5.   Low Self Esteem

A great indication of self-hate is low self-esteem, and it is often demonstrated in the negative vices that again, justify the beliefs that wrong-minded Whites hold about us. Low self-esteem is often the main avenue to doing, saying, being, and pursuing that which is not in one's own best interest. If we thought more of ourselves than we obviously do, no one could compel us to do drugs, break the law, or in any way harm our neighbors or ourselves.

6. Stereotyping

I have touched on the subject of stereotyping several times in this book. That there will be stereotyping, this is not my point of analysis here. My criticism is towards those persons that strive to live up to the stereotypes! If we must live up to stereotypes, let's make it a stereotype of righteousness black men. I remember being stationed at Fort Sill, Oklahoma in 1986. I lost my "Brother Card" because I didn't "play the dozens," walk like my legs were broken, or talk like my mouth were "broken." Then, as if that wasn't bad enough, it was complained to my Platoon Sergeant that I was prejudiced against Black people! I am Black, and though it is possible to be intolerant of your own Race, I was/am not. What did I do or say to make my fellow Black soldiers think I was a hater of my own Black people? I challenged them to be the right kind of men.

"Do you think Martin L. King, Jr. or Malcolm X considered it being Black to talk like we do, or walk like we do?" I asked my accusers. Their silence was my answer.

I do not intend to portray the idea that being like White people is of itself right, but do not reject something simply because it is predominantly White either. I am a Christian, and I do not reject the truths found in Numerology, Satanism, or Darwinism. I reject these ideologies in general, but just as Jesus did not reject the truthful portions of the Devil's try at tempting Him, neither do I reject the points of truth in any system I find.

7. Tradition

Malcolm X pointed out that as African-Americans, "we have always hated ourselves. We hated our hair, we hated the shape of our nose, we hated the color of our skin, because it was stopping us from going this way or that." He added that our belief that the only reason we could not get ahead was because of our Blackness, lead to the natural reaction was to hate that skin, hair and nose, and in fact eventually hating ourselves. We are unable to hate all of our African features and not end up hating ourselves.

Little has changed since the death of Malcolm X, El Hajj Malik El Shabaaz. Today we are still in pursuit of changing the color and texture of our hair, today, the color of our eyes, and the shape of our nose. I would guess right now you are thinking of Michael Jackson, in relationship to even changing the color of our skin. In defense of Mr. Jackson, he does have a skin disorder. I have seen pictures of Michael Jackson at about thirteen years of age where the telltale initial effects of this disorder are visible. I also have a cousin with the same disorder, and her skin looks just like his. If he isn't telling the truth, he has a very plausible fabrication. I am sure no one would blame anyone for having surgery to correct a deformity, or have an unnatural growth removed. A person has to be pitiable to hate what they are to the point of rejecting the very characteristics that make them so individually themselves.

CHAPTER NINE

Uncle Toms and Uncle Sam

One aspect of life for people of color today is the fact that too many times we can't tell if there is genuine racism going on, or merely circumstances that make it appear so. Compiled with that, the well-meaning programs are rejected, twisted, or misunderstood because they are not adequately explained to the public. This lack of communication and misinformation becomes the Achilles heel to any program, leadership, or law intended to correct the problems of race relations in America.

From the inception of this nation the guiding light has supposedly been the Constitution. In the beginning it was actually the White males guiding light, since nonwhite persons were not considered American citizens and White women did not have the same rights of White men. Nonwhite people weren't left out of the Constitution, we just weren't considered human, and therefore, could not claim the same rights as White people under the Constitution. , Article One, Chapter Two, all persons not white shall be considered three fifths of a person. The method of selecting electors is delegated to the separate state legislatures, and the voting procedure to be followed by the electors is carefully defined. Okay let's say it means for census/political reasons only, what did the main author of the Constitution think of nonwhite people?

"The first difference which strikes us is that of color. Whether the black of the Negro resides in the reticular membrane . . . whether it proceeds from the color of the blood, the color of the bile, or from that of some other secretion . . . Is it not the foundation of a greater or less share of beauty in the two races? . . There are other physical distinctions proving a difference of race. . . They are more ardent after their female; but love seems with them to be more an eager desire, than a tender delicate mixture of sentiment and sensation. Comparing them by their faculties of memory, reason, and imagination, it appears to me that in memory they are equal to the whites; in reason much inferior. . . and that in imagination they are dull, tasteless, and anomalous. . . never yet could I find that a black had uttered a thought above the level of plain narration; never saw even an elementary trait of painting or sculpture. In music they are more generally gifted than the whites with accurate ears fortune and time, and they have been found capable of imagining a small catch. . . . I advance it therefore as a suspicion only, that the Black people. . . are inferior to the whites in the endowments of both body and mind." -Thomas Jefferson Notes from the State of Virginia pages 225-226, and 230

We hold these truths to be self-evident that all men are created equal, that they are endowed with certain unalienable rights, life, liberty, and the pursuit of happiness. Oh, the resplendent words, White men have always held personal freedom very high, even declaring give me liberty or give me death. Life, liberty (freedom), and the pursuit of happiness (the ability to seek and enjoy life) according to the Constitution, are rights which were God-given, and could not be taken away by any man! While the words were still being written, the main draftsman of this great document owned over one hundred and twenty five human beings as slaves! Where was the God-given right to freedom and happiness for these men, women, and children? They were deprived of the right to life, freedom, and the opportunity to enjoy that life because they were not considered human beings. They were thought of as animals at best and soul-less property at worst. According to Article one, chapter two, all persons not White shall be considered three fifths of a person. This was later amended, and many people have argued that this three fifths was only for political reasons, but to not be afforded equal representation by government officials was one of the complaints that led to the American Revolution. During and before slavery in America nonwhite people were treated as less than human. This was done in clear conscious because it was done in accord with the Constitution itself. "They amended the Constitution, but they didn't amend the hearts," -Malcolm X. Speaking of the Revolt, consider the Declaration of Independence, which said in part A . . . . whenever any form of government becomes destructive to these ends, it is the right of the people to alter or abolish it and to institute a new government. Just think about that, and ask, "If the government that was supposedly established 'by the people, for the people, under

God," should it not have long ago been replaced by a government that was in more than principle, 'by the people and for the people?" When non-white people where finally considered citizens of America, did the government reflect in it' actions a government for those people? Taxation without true representation shift from Great Britain and the founding fathers to America and Blacks.

CHAPTER TEN

Tricks and Traps

1. Affirmative Action

What may have sounded like a good idea, becomes an albatross around the neck of many Black people. It was clearly known that nonwhites and women were being denied jobs simply because they were nonwhite and/or female. Affirmative Action is the forced acceptance of a certain percentage of people to who because of unfair practices would otherwise not be accepted. The catch is the constant direct and indirect suggestion that persons hired through affirmative action as less than qualified and hired only because of the color of their skin. Now, more than before affirmative action, we must do far more than White workers, students, etc. to prove that we have not been given an undeserved "free ride" or to be accepted as just "close to equal" to our White counterparts.

2. Politics

One of the most enduring tricks of American life is the political machine. In the words of Louis Farrakhan, the problem for Blacks in relation to voting is, "We have always had to choose the lesser of two evils. We have had to choose between the Devil and Satan, and no matter which we pick, we still catch Hell." Whether either major political party has ever done anything in our best interest out of their own sense of moral right is questionable.

3. Republic

(Latin res publica, literally the public thing), form of state based on the concept that sovereignty resides in the people, who delegate the power to rule in their behalf to elected representatives and officials. In practice, however, this concept has been variously stretched, distorted, and corrupted, making any precise definition of the term republic difficult. It is important, to begin with, to distinguish between a republic and a democracy. In the theoretical republican state, where the government expresses the will of the people who have chosen it, republic and democracy may be identical (there are also democratic monarchies). Historical republics, however, have never conformed to a theoretical model, and in the 20th century the term republic is freely used by dictatorships, one-party states, and democracies alike.

4. The Electoral College

Electoral College is the collective name for the electors who nominally choose the president and vice president of the United States. This group comprises the electors from the separate states who are selected by the voters in presidential elections. Each state is entitled to a number of electors equal to the total number of senators and representatives it sends to the U.S. Congress. Thus, each state has at least three electors. Americans pride themselves on living in a Democracy, but the founding father established a Republic, not a Democracy. Secondly, as long as there is the Electoral College, we do not actually have a purely Democratic form of government. Democracy means one man, one vote. The Electoral College means one vote on the behalf of others. Americans do not vote directly for the president, but to tell the representatives at Electoral College for whom they are to vote. If the majority want Politician A, the representative votes for politician A. If the majority want Politician B, the representative votes for Politician B. In theory one would expect it to work, but I would question whether it was ever meant to work. It is a known fact that electors have not always voted for the candidate that received the majority vote?

This is the fear of some Whites: If all people have the right to vote without regard to color, gender, etc., the majority rules. If the persons in charge do not want to lose their positions of power, they must devise a scheme in which the people have no real say in who will be in charge. Even though they have the right to vote, it doesn't matter who they vote for. The votes cast by The Electoral College are the deciding factor on who will be the president. If you don't think it is conceivable, an important change resulted from a serious dispute in the presidential election of 1876. Republican, Rutherford B. Hayes, and the Democrat, Samuel J. Tilden, were the candidates. The dispute involved the validity of the electoral votes of four states, and the outcome was crucial, since Tilden needed just one of the 22 votes to have a majority and Hayes needed all 22 to win. Under existing law, it was the duty of Congress to resolve the dispute, but Congress found itself deadlocked. Finally, the issue was settled through the creation of the Electoral Commission of 1877, which chose Hayes on a strict party vote, eight to seven. Later, in 1887, Congress enacted a law that gave the states almost exclusive power to resolve all controversies regarding the selection of presidential electors and that made mandatory, except in cases in which electors vote irregularly, the acceptance by Congress of all certificates of election duly made by the states. The enactment also provided that Congress might intervene to settle a dispute over the election of the presidential electors of a state only when the state is unable to do so.

5. Propaganda

The systematic, widespread promotion of a certain set of ideas, doctrines, etc., especially to further one's own cause. There has been seemingly overt propaganda against people of color almost since our emancipation from slavery. The media constantly portrays nonwhite people in a negative light. Portrayals from cartoons to million dollar movies, we are fed a constant diet of racial bias. Radio commentator, Rush Limbaugh, found it hard to believe that someone would purposely misrepresent the number of theater tickets purchased for Spike Lee's movie, Malcolm X. The claim was that the tickets sold for Malcolm X, registered in the computer as other movies in the theater system. I remembered his initial doubt when later Mr. Limbaugh's first book came out in print. Someone programmed the computers at certain bookstores to read the bar code for his book as another book he had not written.

In the media, nonwhites may be reported as having committed certain offenses, while the White persons are only alleged to have committed certain illegal acts.

6. Welfare

Possibly second only to crime, welfare rates high on the list of tricks. Even nonwhite people think of nonwhites when the term welfare is spoken. The propaganda machine is so brazen that even inside the Welfare Offices there are posters depicting minority women almost exclusively. In reality, there have been at times, more Whites on welfare than nonwhite! Statistics may vary from state to state but welfare is definitely not an exclusive club for nonwhites. This means in all actuality, so-called minorities are not lazy after. In reality, most minorities choose poor wages over welfare, but you may not be able to convince a racist this is true.

CHAPTER ELEVEN

Do All Roots Stem From Africa?

Whether one accepts creationism or the theory of evolution, most people concede that life originated on the continent we know today as Africa. Regardless of the color or shades, both the Bible and science agree that Africa is the motherland of all mankind. Do not be surprised that science and religion agree. There is agreement between science and the Bible everywhere science tells the truth. If it is true that White people share a common genetic heritage with Black people science would support the single origin of mankind, if not the story creation itself.

The assertion is that we are all the descendants of Adam and Eve, monkeys, or Anthropomorphic of some type. The question then is, "Where did all the races or different colors originate?" It would be easy to assume that if the story of the Tower of Babel is true; all the people of the world that spoke the same language naturally grouped together and went out to dwell in the same regions.

On the other hand, there is reason to believe that the Genesis story gives the creation of at least two groups of people. According to the Bible at Genesis 2:7 God created man from the dust of the earth. He then created woman from the man's rib, according to Genesis 2:21-23. Later in the Genesis story, Cain, one of two sons to the first man and woman, is banished for killing his brother Abel. Cain left to dwell in the land of Nod, where he met and married his wife. It is here that most Christians, theologians and atheists find a great problem with the Bible as truth revealed from God. They ask, "Where did Cain get his wife?"

"The Bible doesn't say. He must have married his sister, but incest was okay then. God knows, and it is not necessary for our salvation to know. We will know when we get to Heaven. I don't know," are usually the inadequate answers given. Any person is right to ask, but is the Bible silent on this point? The answer is a resounding "No!" There are several things misunderstood about the book of Genesis, or missed all together. Genesis 1:27-28 states that God made humankind, not a singular man, but as the term male and female, and the plural pronoun them refers. In Genesis 2:2, all the work of creation is done and God rests. In the following verses of that same chapter we recognize God's chosen man: Adam. He is to be the example for all of mankind, and a precursor of Jesus the Christ.

According to the Bible at I Corinthians 15:45 this man, was a foreshadow of Jesus the Christ. Adam and his wife are sanctified, or set apart from the rest of humankind, and placed in a garden to the east in Eden. The theme of a chosen person or people reoccurs throughout the Bible. Adam and Eve were the first chosen among all the people that God created. The Jewish people were chosen, and today the Christians are God's chosen John 15:16, Ephesians 1:4, and I Peter 2:9.

Cain, after leaving Eden, dwelt in the land of Nod. Cain did not name nod, but by those who inhabited the area before he reached it. The city that Cain founded was named Enoch after his first son. Subsequently, Cain speaks at Genesis 4:14 stating that, "everyone that seeth me, which sounds like someone other than his parents or other relatives as some have surmised.

The most compelling evidence for the creation of others in addition to Adam and Eve is found at Genesis 5:1-2. The Hebrew word Adam here, is a literal translation for the word mankind. This explanation can be found in the King James, and New Oxford Standard Annotated Bible. When we view the scriptures with an open, but honest mind, the truth not only leaps from the pages, but the light of that truth illuminates the lies that have been fed about religion.

The inescapable fact is that Cain met and married a woman that lived in the land of Nod, and we have no scriptural reason to believe that she was his sister. It is not important for our salvation, to know where and who the inhabitants of Nod were, but ignorance about such trivial points as where did Cain get his wife will cast doubt on the rest of the word of God and conceivably even man's belief in God Himself. It imperative for this reason that we know the truth for ourselves and not make up excuses and elaborate tales to cover our lack of knowledge.

The other people beside Adam and Eve may very well point to the original inhabitants of Europe. This could count for the difference in skin color. It may be that the mark that was set upon Cain, was not necessarily new to him, but new to the people he would meet. The first Black man in Europe would automatically be set apart or different from the inhabitants of Europe. It was not that God made Cain Black after he killed his brother, it was that there were the different shades of Black and he was not set apart until he was at the point of coming into contact with others who were not Black people also.

If a Black person marries a White person, what color will the child be? According to the United States government, the child is considered to be Black. After all, (in line with the mind of Adolph Hitler) the child can't be White; it is tainted, impure, mixed, even if it has only one to six percent Black blood! So staunch is this belief that the government has refused to allow a White grandmother to adopt her inter-racial grandchild because the child is Black.

CHAPTER TWELVE

The Invention of Race

Men have debated, argued, and honestly questioned of the origin of the differing skin colors. The core question is, "Why are people different colors?" There are many people that share the same features and accents that are different colors. There are many people that place a heavy emphasis on the color of a person's skin, and answers range from a curse from God to, mere adaptation to climate.

1. Adam and Zinj-Anthropus

The Holy Bible records the creation of mankind (Adam) at Genesis 1: 26-28. We can read of the specific creation of the first man, Adam at 2:7-15 in Africa. The evidence is the naming of Ethiopia, Euphrates, and Tigris, all of which are in Africa.

Under the Theory of Evolution, British paleoanthropologist Dr. Louis Leakey searched for the origin of mankind. He found his end and man's beginning on the continent of Africa. The remains Dr. Leakey named Zin Anthropus. Zin means black, and Anthropus meaning man. The oldest known remains of mankind, where found in what is referred to as The Cradle of Civilization.

2. Tower of Babel

Given the fact that no group or "race" of people has any one set of physical characteristics, would it not be understandable to assign the different languages to the groups that shared common characteristics. Those who shared Mongoloid characteristics shared the Asian language, while those who share the more darkened skin we know as African, shared the African dialect. If the Bible is correct at Corinthians 14:33, "God is not the author of confusion," then it would support the idea that even in the babbling at the tower, there was a method to the madness.

3. Yacub

Then, leader of the Nation of Islam, Elijah Muhammad taught that a great scientist was responsible for engineering a new race of people through the intermarrying of light skinned people. As his followers continued his plans, which resulted in the creating of the White race.

According to the Nation of Islam teaching, long ago there were only Black people on the earth. A great scientist named Yacub decided to create a new race of people. This was prophesied, and the king knew it would happen. The king and Yacub agreed to him and his followers leaving for another land where Yacub continued with his plans. The scientists mated light skinned people with each other, and even after Yacub died, the experiment continued until the light skinned people developed into what we know today as the Caucasian race came into being.

In time the Anew race came to hate the original, Blacks, secluding themselves in the caves of Europe and the area known today as the Caucus Mountains. Minister Farrakhan points out that after generations of living in the dark caves of Europe, the White people adapted to their surroundings, and grew excessive amounts of hair, took on the characteristics of animals, and developed bad postures from continuous stooping. Minister Farrakhan added, the hip area widens, and the eyes lighten. Then there are also the abhorrent curse stories:

4. Hams Curse

One of the most diabolical lies of false Christianity is the teaching that Noah's son was cursed with black skin, and condemned to servitude. It is recorded in the Bible at Genesis chapter nine that the waters of the flood had subsided. Noah's son, Ham came upon him in a drunken state. Apparently his clothing was disheveled and his nakedness was in view. Rather than cover his father, Ham left him and reported it to his brothers, Shem and Japeth. In the Patriarchal Age of the Bible, this was a show of disrespect on Ham's part. Later, under the Mosaic Law, as noted at Deuteronomy 27:26, it was a sin for the Jews to show contempt towards ones parents. It was also a sin to uncover the nakedness of a parent according to Leviticus 18:6-7. In verse 25 Noah declared, cursed be Canaan; a servant of servants shall he be unto his brethren. Canaan was the first son of Ham and the punishment of Ham was visited upon Canaan. The punishment was servitude, not black skin. The only rationale for this supposed curse is the fact that the descendants of Ham, Canaan, Cush, and Sheba, for are admitted by White scholars to be Black! Rather than fully admit to the Blackness of the people of the Bible, they make the obvious truths to be something abnormal, as if a White Noah's descendants were turned black. This racist thinking is almost a carbon copy of Mormon doctrines on race. When a person lies, he must either tell another lie to support it, or it uncovers another truth. If our blackness makes us descendants of Noah's son's, then they and we by lineage are the "original people."

5. Mormonism

Many White so-called Christian ministers have preached, and continue to preach that because of a curse from his father, Noah, Hams descendants were made Black and inferior. It is not surprising to hear that was taught during the days of slavery in America. It may be surprising to some though, to learn that it is not just alluded to in sermons and thought, but written in sufficient detail in the Book of Mormon, which is claimed by the Church of Jesus Christ of Latter Day Saints to be from God. If that book were actually from God, then Jesus Christ Himself would have been under the same curse because of His Blackness. Christ would according to racist doctrine, would have to be disobedient to God, mischievous in mind, and lazy since this is what the Book of Mormon attributes to all Black people.

I Nephi 12:22-23

"And it came to pass that I beheld, that they had dwindled in unbelief they became a dark, and loathsome, and filthy people, full of idleness and all manner of abominations."

II Nephi 5:21-24

"And he had caused the curse to come upon them, yea, even a sore cursing, because of their iniquity. For behold, they had hardened their hearts against him, that they had become like unto a flint; wherefore, as they were white, and exceedingly fair and delightsome, that they might not be enticing unto my people the Lord God did cause a skin of blackness to come upon thee.

22 And thus saith the Lord God: I will cause that they shall be loathsome unto thy people, save they shall repent of their iniquities.

23 And cursed shall be the seed of him that mixeth with their seed; for they shall be cursed even with the same cursing. And the Lord spake it and it was done.

24 And their cursing which was upon them they did become and idle people full of mischief and subtlety, and did seek in the wilderness for beasts of prey."

I was once told that my white wife was black by injection. Is it true that in every joke there is a little truth? In this case their truth is that sexual relations with a black man, makes a white woman black, that is to say, "impure."

Alma 3:6-10

"And the skins of the Lamanites were dark, according to the mark which was set upon their fathers, which was a curse upon them because of their transgressions and their rebellion against their brethren, who consisted of Nephi, Jacob that whosoever did mingle his seed with that of the Lamanites did bring the same curse upon his seed.

10 Therefore, whosoever suffered himself to be led away by the Lamanites was called under that head, and there was a mark set upon him."

Jacob 3:5, 8-9

5. "Behold the Lamanites your brethren, whom you hate because of their filthiness and the cursing which hath come upon their skins.

8. O my brethren, I fear that unless ye shall repent of your sins that their skins will be whiter than yours, before the throne of God.

9 Wherefore, a commandment I give unto you, which is the word of God, that ye revile no more against them because of the darkness of their skins; neither shall ye revile against them because of their filthiness."

With an honest investigation it becomes unarguably evident that the Christian Bible is the word of God. With that, any writings that claim to also be the word of God must either correlate with the Bible or be a lie. Claiming that God turned beautiful Whites into ugly, evil, Black people is far beyond even the distortions of the Bible embellished by the slave owners of the South.

CHAPTER THIRTEEN

From Niger to Nigger

"Another can judge a criminal case as well as I. What I would like to do is to correct the conditions that bring that criminal case about."-Confucius

Even the very least of us can point out what's wrong with society and relationships as they associate to racism. The challenge for humanity is to engineer a solution and be a part of that solution, rather than a part of the problem. Here are some areas where we can do to be a part of the solution:

1. Demeanor

It does matter what other people think of you! If you don't believe me, try getting a job at a prestigious firm, bank, hotel, etc. dressed like a homeless person. Try getting Public Assistance while dressed, and acting like a millionaire. People do judge books by their covers, and first impressions can be lasting. Unless you, or those who have your best interest in mind, control labor, law, and education, you will have to conform to what the leaders in these fields consider acceptable, or exist outside mainstream society.

2. Bitterness

Actor Denzel Washington said of his starring in the movie, Malcolm X, I became very angry. After the ordeal I suffered at the hands of my racist leaders, I can relate. The racial incident with them was not my first encounter with racism, but it was the closest I ever came to hating in return. When we realize, or truly reflect upon the way things have been and the way they are now, it can easily stir up feelings of bitterness. This is especially true for those of us who have looked at the things we have had to put up with as Black people. What we must do is redirect our bitterness, transform the emotion of anger into pity. It is a shame that any person would miss out on all that relationships with differing humans has to offer merely because of skin color. I am so thankful that my parents never attempted to instill in me a racist mind set.

3. Crime

Don't do crimes! When the time comes that Black people don't commit crimes, then no innocent Black person should be arrested, harassed, or held under deep suspicion for what another Black person has done. Decent White police officers will be at ease when approaching Black men; this will be a relief on the part of Black civilians and police officers alike. Also we will be able to open the eyes of "Lady Justice," enabling her to see that because Black people don't commit crimes, therefore a Black person must now be considered innocent until proven guilty before the courts of law.

4. Education

There are many books on achieving practically anything one might desire. All we have to do is get and use a library card! Why waste time with trial and error, when we can just read what mistakes others have made in pursuit of the same goals you have. Learn from their mistakes rather than wasting time, money, and effort on trial and error attempts at success.

When the mind is positively stimulated and becomes more analytical, it becomes easier to arrive at answers to life's problems. Riots have occurred when people, fed up with injustice felt they could find no other way to vent their frustrations. We strike out violently and criminally rather than intelligently and methodically because we have not become accustomed to using our mental faculties.

5. Ignorance

I blame no one for not knowing something, but with access to almost anything dealing with knowledge, wisdom, or learning, via free libraries, and now the Internet, there is no reason to remain ignorant. Even in the Bible we find a limit to the extent of acceptable ignorance.

"Where there was a time of such ignorance, God winked at, but now is the time for all men to come to repentance." Acts 17:30.

6. Inferiority Complex

The amount of self-esteem we hold is reflected in our actions. As long as we think little of ourselves in a degrading manner, we will act and react in a degrading manner. When we act and react in a self-appreciating manner, it will also show in how we dress, speak, and carry ourselves in a more respectable way.

Cyclically, we will think more highly of ourselves when we carry ourselves better. Thinking more highly of ourselves should lead to increasing our mental capabilities through study, and analytical reasoning on all levels. As this new attitude and defining of Blackness occurs, the world will eventually see it, and see us in a better light. With the educating of the "nigger," we bring about the destruction of the nigger, and like an ugly cocoon that yields a beautiful butterfly; the real Black man will emerge. Then like the Preacher man shouts, "Weeping may endure for a night, but joy cometh in the morning!" The weeping of change yields the joy of being a beneficial part of society instead of a leach, or blight, which is rejected by the mainstream society. The Black man becomes awakened and we will be men and women, not Niggers!

7.   Social Status

Once we see how raising our self-esteem can raise our thinking, we can also see our social status will change. With the mind in us, we will open doors of opportunity that we once kept closed on ourselves. Once those doors of opportunity are opened, monetary rewards and success will follow. The intelligent use of money will lift our social status, where the ignorant misuse of it has in past, failed those nonwhite celebrities and sports figures. Raise your self-esteem and your mind, and body will follow.

As Black people become sanctified, or lifted up mentally and financially, we can help other nonwhites achieve the same, and when we as a people are living out our potential, there will truly be no longer niggers! Then it will be clear that anyone that calls us niggers will obviously be lying. When our minds and bodies are sanctified, we will cease to be niggers!

8. Stereotyping

We may never stop the stereotyping of Black people, but we can inhibit the negative stereotyping first by not acting out the very stereotypes that are generally depicted in the media and society. Rather than mimic the thugs, and criminals, lets mimic the greatest Black man that ever walked the face of the earth: Jesus Christ.

I say, "Let's create the stereotype of Black men and women as righteous, then live up to that stereotype." When we become righteous, seeing us all as righteous will not be a stereotype, it will be an accurate assessment of all Black people. Let's live the life of Christians as God intended us to, then He will truly be with us and we will begin to see what the world can be like when men live righteously, rather than what it is now as a result of unrighteousness.

9. Superiority Complex

In Islam there is a parable about an angel named Iblis. The story goes that Allah created all the angels then man. After creating man He commanded the angels to bow down to man. All of the angels bowed except Iblis. Allah asked him, why he did not bow.

Iblis said, "He (man) is made from dirt, I am made from fire. I cannot bow to him; I am better than he."

To this, Allah replied, "Didn't I make dirt, and didn't I make fire, what did stop you, if I commanded you to bow?"

Again Iblis answered, "I cannot bow to him, I am better." The moral of the parable is that when we think we are better than someone else simply because of some unique characteristic about ourselves, we become as devils. Do not marvel at the reference to evil people as devils, long before Malcolm X, The Book of Mormon referred to evil people as devils, and their reference was specifically to evil, white people.

10. Tradition

"If we forget the past, we are doomed to repeat it," is a famous quote, but whether it is regarded is questionable. We should not disregard our past, but instead apply our knowledge of history in a more beneficial manner. We must not use slavery and its repercussions as crutches. We must remember that there is a chance for history to repeat itself, if we make the same mistakes that our ancestors made. I do not believe our African ancestors would have sold their brothers into American slavery if they had any clue what was in store for them. Most slaves in Africa were treated as little more than stepchildren. Even unwanted stepchildren are not broken like wild horses. They do not have portions of live ant beds shoveled into their opened abdomen. They are not torn apart by two horses going in opposite directions. They are not beaten mercilessly because they cried at the death of a fellow slave.

We are still suffering the effects of slavery, because of certain racist traditions, this can't be honestly denied. Both Black people and Whites suffer, because of lies and the reaction to these lies. People still believe the racist themes and react to them accordingly. We are still singing "steal away to Jesus, steal away home," but today we do not know that the slaves were not singing Gospel. The Jesus they wanted to steal away to was the slave ship Jesus, and home was Africa. If we live with the tradition of staying in our place then we are doomed to continue in mental slavery.

Tradition for the sake of tradition based on "we has always done it this way," or "This is just the way it has always been," is no longer acceptable. African-Americans have a traditional diet that should be rejected. Caucasians have a tradition of Iblis, which should be rejected. I am glad to see that the younger generations are no longer willing to fight the illegitimate battles of their fore fathers. The open minded White youth are purging the racist minds of the past as sanctified minds of young Black people are destroying the mind of servitude that for too long has been common among people of color.

11. Subconscious Heredity

We can empower our subconscious by empowering our conscious mind. Most can do little to change the world because they have accepted inferiority it contains. If we change our conscious attitudes and beliefs, the mind of inferiority will be purged and the original mind of greatness will replace it.

If you don't think the mind of self-destruction is in the mind of Black people, explain the fact that when the Black Messiah came we killed him. Of course not you and I literally, but the very people He came to save, were the same that called for His crucifixion. Of course the Jewish leaders had money and power to lose at the rise of the Messiah, but why did the masses follow them? We had not changed in 1965 when Malcolm X was gunned down in front of his family by the very men he had dedicated his life to helping. Again, they had their own vested interests, both Jesus and Malcolm's death were in vein if we do not live up to the good things that they began for us. This holds true for every martyr, whether he is as noted Martin Luther King; Jr. or as remote as Joe Shmo who died as a result of wounds suffered during freedom rides into Mississippi.

Our savior, the Messiah, Jesus the Christ, lived the life He preached and He was killed for it. Would we also kill our intellectual messiah, our social messiah, or economic messiah? If we would receive him, rather than reject him, our people could be saved intellectually, socially, and economically?

Remember that with unity, we have power! One drop of rain on the frailest flower will do it no harm. A torrent of raindrops though, united and moving in the same direction can carve valleys, and reshape mountains. Just as a roaring flood can destroy manmade structures, Black people united for good, can change wrongly concocted man made organizations, and injustice.

Do we nonwhite people have a working knowledge of politics, economics, world trade, etc. to keep the "American Machine" humming along? The sad truth is, the Whites in charge, are barely holding on to the system of things as they exist today. Too many Americans do not care to see past their own noses. If their own little domain is not upset, noticeably, they do not care to look into anything outside what seems to be their span of control. I say, "Seems to be" because the reality of life is that we do not have control of much that we believe we do.

12. Police Yourselves

Police- 1. The regulation of morals, safety, etc., 2. The duty of keeping an area clean and orderly. I read a short exposition:

"When they came for the Jews, I said nothing because I wasn't Jewish.

When they came for the Black people, I said nothing because I wasn't Black.

When they came for the homosexuals, I said nothing because I wasn't homosexual.

When they came for me, there was no one left to say anything."

If we wait to be affected by injustice before we decide to do anything about it, will that be too late. Dr. King said, injustice anywhere is a threat to justice everywhere. I have heard it said on many occasions, by Black people as well as Whites that there will always be racism. Well if we accept that, then yes, there will always be racism. On the other hand, if good White people stand up against villainous White people, they can help influence a change. Someone once said, "All it takes for evil to rein, is for good people to do nothing." Based on this truism, understand that most people want to be accepted by their peers. If people know that their wrong thinking will ostracize them from society, they will change their minds and/or actions. At the same time Whites are affecting Whites, good Black people should be doing the same with our fellow Black people harboring reverse racist thinking. If the only outcome is a polarization of these two classes, haters and acceptors, then so be it. We have always had segregation, but under these circumstances, all of humankind can now benefit from it.

CHAPTER FOURTEEN

Raising the Black Mahdi

People throughout history have looked for a type of Messiah, savior, leader, or Mahdi, to do for them that which they could not find in themselves to do! I don't think it's wrong to look to a righteously guided person, but what would we do with a modern Messiah or Mahdi? If history still repeats itself, we will accept him initially, hoping he will guide us to what we want with no compulsion toward us to be righteous. When we have gotten all we can without submission to righteousness, we will then reject and look for the opportunity to destroy him?

The Bible as well as history itself, records that Jesus of Nazareth was accepted by the masses who hoped he would lead them to the establishment of a national homeland. In the end, even the disciple that said he would die for him repudiated him. He was deserted even though he had earlier been received as if he were a king. When the time came to choose between Jesus and a criminal, the crowd called for Barabbas. History repeated itself in 1965 when Malcolm X was assassinated by men he had dedicated himself to trying to help bring out of the bondage of mental darkness. The men would choose the so-called Honorable Elijah Muhammad over the publicly transformed and now well-intentioned Malcolm. As a misguided Minister of the Nation of Islam, Malcolm was instrumental in the conversion of literally thousands of people to the Nation of Islam. He was lauded and revered until he abandoned the false doctrine that all Whites are inherently evil. Ironically when he rejected the racist doctrine and called for righteousness, he himself was rejected and killed by his own.

Today we need not wait for the rise of another Black Messiah. We must ourselves, raise the Black Mahdi. The Black Mahdi must not be a single man that leads us, but our collective consciousness that through unity raises us up! In the Bible at Genesis 5:2 for example, the word Adam is used synonymously for the first man and mankind. I would like to see the term Mahdi used in the same way. Rather than one righteous or rightly guided being, let's all become righteous and rightly guided by God through His word, the Bible.

Single men, (Malcolm, Martin, Gandhi, etc.) have been too easily killed, but we as a people, cannot be so easily and completely destroyed, unless God, Himself destroys us! Because of our disobedience we have been destroyed, that is cut off spiritually from God, but He desires to receive us again.

Truly, "United we stand, divided we fall." What would happen if all the nonwhites disappeared tomorrow? What if only the African-Americans disappeared? Would it cause a drastic change in America, or would life go on barely interrupted and the exodus of the Black masses go almost unnoticed? Would corporations teeter on the verge of collapse or the economy reel from the effects of this loss?

What would happen if all the Caucasian people of America disappeared? Imagine the tumult of not having the leaders of America, the decision-makers, the loss would be catastrophic. As long as there aren't enough nonwhites in positions of power and prominence to run the show we really aren't that significant.

With the loss of Black people, replacement of the "twos and fews" that matter in the grand scheme would be relatively easy. On the other hand to lose the majority of the people who actually control the wires that make sure America still continues, as we know it. The remaining people may or may not be skilled in the areas that are necessary to stave off a veritable apocalypse. We need them, if only because they are the controlling forces that holds the American system together. They don't need us, and if we disappeared today, it would barely affect life, as they have it. I'm also aware that the decent White people that are true friends and friendly would feel a loss, but their lives would not be in danger of collapse. In the words of Malcolm X, I hate to say this about us, but it's true.

Who of color will step forward and be the leader of this country as the Black Mahdi for this age? Former Army General Colon Powell had the chance, but even when the Reform Party attempted to force him to run for the US presidency, he declined.

He said, "Don't give me the job, I didn't apply for it." While he refused to return to government service for the good of Black people (specifically as an example to Black youth) he returned to government service at the request of newly elected President Bush, Jr. for "the benefit of the country." Not only did he not run for office, which would have been an inspiration even if he had lost, he left the volunteer organization which he was a part of. How quick we are to sacrifice for others and leave our own wanting. You'll fight for the White man, but when it comes to seeing your own Black girls blown to bits, you don't have any fight. The words of Malcolm X ring out almost prophetically for former General Powell, who by the nature of his job was willing to put his life on the line in the Armed Services, but not in a bid for leadership of America.

Must we be forced to "raise up" leaders by the failure of the conventional leadership of this country? If so, what are we training our sons and daughters to be? Are we preparing and encouraging them to take a role in the leadership of their school, neighborhood, city, town, state, country, and even the world? Are we telling them to merely graduate from school, get a good job, and "try to make it?" Are we teaching them that they should be happy to receive the crumbs and go unaccented by mainstream America?

"Are we instead, teaching our children to become so powerfully independent that they don't need the crumbs of socialism that America hands out in the form of Welfare to its minorities?"

"Are we raising our children to be niggers? Do we condone and promote our daughters doing the "hootchie mamma" dance, or do we promote modest womanhood? Do we encourage the intellectual development of our sons, or do we tell them to prepare their bodies for a life of menial labor?"

Raising the Black Mahdi and self-dependence are so important and yet unrealized. Let's start small and work our way up. For example if we had our own restaurant, we could care less if Denny's Restaurant did not want us eating there, we could simply eat in our own restaurants! Personally, I don't think we should have in the past, present, or future, force our way into another man's establishment. He put his hard work and money into his business, and he should have the right to serve whomever he wants. We would never think of forcing our way into someone's home would we? If a group of people don't want us in their neighborhood, let's establish our own neighborhoods. If someone doesn't want us in his or her state, let us establish our own state! Let us establish our own schools, businesses, hospitals, everything that we bow down to receive from people that don't want to share with us what they have amassed for themselves. I'm not a Black Muslim, or a Black Separatist, but my mother and common sense taught me that if someone doesn't want me around them, I shouldn't be around them. If someone gives, sells, or allows me to have something begrudgingly, I don't want it. If you don't want me in brotherhood, friendship and as a fellow human being I wish you well, and that you would find a place for yourself with yourself. When the government has to force White establishments (in the year 2000) to serve Blacks rather than it being free acceptance our patronage we do not have true integration and freedom.

In the Greek expression of agape, I love White people, just as I love nonwhite people. I love the stimulating conversation, I love the friendly debates about history, politics, and religion, and in all honesty, I even like pointy noses, and cleft chins. In spite of those physical, and mental characteristics, I do not wish to be with those who don't want to be with me. I leave them to their own, the racists, White supremacist, and such. I warn them, "Don't try to destroy me simply because I'm Black." One day they may just realize that every time they destroy a man desiring to change this world for good, simply because of his color, they endanger their own well-being as well as that of their children's! This is my hope.

I don't expect the stripping of the slave mentality can be done in one lifetime, but the striping must continue. It started with men like Marcus Garvey, Malcolm X, and Huey P. Newton, but it must continue. I know that as with like-minded men, I probably won't be alive to see it brought into existence, but I must do my part to see that it is begun. To echo Malcolm X from the Oxford Debate of 1964, "I will join with anyone; I don't care what color you are. As long as you want to change the miserable condition that exists on this earth."

If we don't look into ways to change the world, it will never be changed for the better, it will only get worse. Evidence to this is that the same racism leveled against nonwhite people in 1950, 1960, 1970, 1980, and 1990 still exists. Admittedly not to the same degree, and not as open and frequently. In the year 2000 only one Black man's being "anally" violated by policemen is too many. How many Black people can be shot over 40 times before justice is "shaken awake" to the plight of nonwhite people of America and the world? How many more Black men need to be dragged to their death behind a pickup truck, and how many more church fires will be enough? Black people can still be arrested and lost, stopped and searched because of the color of their skin. We are still denied decent jobs, homes, or an equal chance at the American Dream. I dare anyone to prove me wrong, because I have the facts on my side. Undeniable evidence as near as the news, not just well articulated rhetoric.

How to Help Strip the Slave Mind of Adults:

1. Good people of all races must take an unyielding and boisterous stand against prejudice based on skin color, national origin, sex, or religion.

2. Black people must stop being niggers! (It is not the dip in your walk, the filth in your talk, or the unique way you wear clothes that make you black!) We cannot give justification for white racism by our ignorant acts of violence, unintelligent speaking and unlearned behavior; this is our part in ending racism.

3. White people must accept the undeniable truth that mankind originated in Africa, and whether one accepts the Theory of evolution, or creation by an all-powerful God, the first man raised his face to the sun in Africa! This is theological, anthropological, and historical fact. If all men are descendants from the first man who was black, no one can claim to be better than present-day black men because all men are black! Like the angel Iblis, we Black men cannot claim to be better than the White man because we didn't have anything to do with our Blackness. Coffee with a lot of creamer is no better than coffee straight. It only tastes a little different, but it is still coffee, regardless of the color. If God

did made Caucasians apart from Blacks, we are still the entire same human race.

4. The prosecution to the fullest extent of the law, those persons who are found guilty of hate crimes must be assured! When the fear of the law is brought back, men will respect and keep the law! This is evidenced by the fact that Japanese police until recently did not carry guns, but Japan has one of the lowest crime rate in the world!

5. Admittedly, the best hope for the world is to set the youngest members of our human race on the path to a better tomorrow. We must refrain from passing our wrongly guided precepts to the children. The adults seem to be content having the crumbs of Americanism, or do not have any hope for the future. They are not living, they merely exist. Furthermore, racism has not made America better, so let them try love for future generations. Will your hatred for fellow men be stronger than the desire to see children live in a better world? I ask, "Even if Whites were superior to nonwhites, wouldn't the world be better without the hatred of those you deem inferior to yourselves?" Lady Justice is blind to justice for nonwhites, but there will be a Black man whose return will right all the wrongs of this world. I know this because, as it is written in God's word, so shall it be done. Thomas Jefferson knew it too because he said, I tremble for my country when I reflect that God is just; that his justice cannot sleep forever. Mr. Jefferson may have trembled, but still he did not repent!

CHAPTER FIFTEEN

Why We Don't Die of Old Age

A giant sea turtle can move rapidly through in water, but is painfully slow on land. Unfortunately, things are established in nature so that the sea turtle must go inland to lay her eggs. The shallow grave-like nests are prepared and the mother turtle goes back to the sea. When the eggs hatch, and the baby turtles begin their short (from our human perspective) migration to the sea. The safety of the sea is not close enough for some of the unfortunate young who are picked off by predators before reaching the refuge of the water.

Black families are at times, very much like those sea turtles. When we were in our own element of wisdom, unity, and most of all obedience to God, we were the "masters of our own destiny," and rulers of the known world. Foolishly turning our back on God, we were taken from the safety and order of life in Africa, to be chastised with the tumultuous history of slavery in America. Continuing in disobedience our young men and women are sent from the home into public schools and society. Here as they make their way "to and fro," they are attacked by predators known as drugs, illicit sex, gangs, racism, and substandard education, to name a few. In the movie Billy Jack, actor Tom Laughlin speaks to local policemen who were about to begin illegally shooting wild mustangs. "When policemen break the law, then there isn't any law, just a fight for survival."

In the world of Billy Jack, the policemen were stopped, but reality is not a movie in which wrongs are so easily corrected. For instance, White children are taught that the police are their friends, and that they should be sought out if the child finds himself in need of help. The Black child comes to see the police as the enemy at worst, and not to be trusted, at best. I am a reasonably intelligent, fifty-six-year-old, Black man. and I would like to believe that the police are there "to protect and to serve." Unfortunately too many times when the curtains are pulled back and we can look behind the scenes, I am convinced that many men wearing badges do not have nonwhite people's best interest at heart.

I remember an episode of a certain weekly news show, in which they were looking into the hanging death of a teenage African-American. The teen had supposedly hung himself with his own belt from the window of his jail cell, after his arrest following a routine traffic check. The problems with the supposed suicide is the fact that this teen, an amateur of habit, never wore a belt, and the window of his solitary cell was too high for him to reach. That may seem circumstantial, but the coroner found clear evidence that a thin cord was used to strangle the youth! Yet another example of the taking of a Black man's life, and this was not done in the nineteen-sixty, it was done in the nineteen-eighties.

I was taking my then, seven-year-old daughter to the dentist one morning when we pulled up alongside a police cruiser. I wanted to tell her, Wave to the nice policeman, but I did not want to be embarrassed by a negative reaction from the officer, thus inadvertently giving my daughter the chance to develop a negative attitude toward the police, as I had. I accept the fact that like any group of people, there are good and bad police officers. I have been fortunate enough to meet some of the good ones, but I have to consciously fight against the impression of what seems to be the majority. I hope we are wrong in our opinion of police. Their part is to be good cops, and our part is to allow them the opportunity to be good cops, mainly, by not breaking the law. As good cops, they have to stand up against bad cops that may not seem to directly affect them. In reality good cops are affected by bad cops just as good Blacks are affected by bad Blacks. The policeman I saw may very well have been a good cop, but he missed a chance to have a positive experience because of the legacy of bad cops.

During an Equal Opportunity class, I met a White military police person (female) who related to me that she heard some type of racial or sexist remark from her coworkers at least once a week! Not only did she stand for it, but the members of our EO staff whom she also spoke to, stood for it! When the agencies supposedly established for the wellbeing of all people do nothing to correct the negative effects of racism, not only do they become a waste of time, money, and manpower, but they share a collective guilty in the injustices meted out in America.

If we do nothing to stop an action, we inadvertently help that action to be successful. Perhaps these entities were established merely to lull minorities into thinking someone is looking out for them? This concept is not unheard of when you research the debacles known as the Korean War, the Vietnamese War, Communism, and the Middle East crisis. The previous failures of America are examples of how the stated aims were not accomplished because the actual intent was never to accomplish the published goals in the first place! In Korea General Macarthur learned this, in Vietnam, South Vietnamese soldiers knew this. In Korea, when America urged them to transfer a portion their land into Communist hands they knew it, and in the Middle East the people that accept millions in American subsidy to include war machines, yet still do not acquiesce American requests know that stated aims and secret aims are not always the same. Lastly, even Russia is aware of the fact that America's national symbol should not be the sharp-eyed eagle, but the two-faced, Janus! Tragically, even the aid to Africa comes under question when as Malcolm X pointed out, "They can't help Blacks right here in America, they have to send all the way to Africa to help." As pointed out earlier, no one does a good deed simply for the sake of doing a good deed. So what does America gain from helping Africa? I assure you that it isn't the warm fuzzy feeling of "I have done a good deed." Don't misunderstand me, I am sure that the masses of followers feel good about helping, but I doubt the leadership's intentions are honorable. One of the most powerful religious entities in existence is the Catholic Church. I have conversed with several Catholics who do not believe in praying directly to Mary or that she is co-redeemer with Jesus, but you just ask the Pope what Mary's role in Catholicism is! There is even a branch of study called Mariology! Another point many practicing Catholics do not know.

Don't think I am attacking Catholics or making example of them exclusively. Black Muslims who reject that Jehovah God came in the person of the man Jesus Christ because God cannot become man, do not reject the NOI doctrine that Allah God came in the person of WD Farrad.

CHAPTER SIXTEEN

Some of the Greatest Lies Ever Told

American author Elbert Hubbard wrote, "A man found in the South Sea Islands a tribe of savages so meager in intelligence that they could not lie. However, there were neighboring islands where missionaries of several denominations had settled. And there the savages were not sunk quite so low."

I suppose the White missionaries on the other island had taught the savages on their island how to lie. Imagine equating intelligence with the ability to lie! I suppose that makes genius of some White people based some of the great lies they have told:

LIE #1. Black Skin is A Curse From God.

TRUTH: Most of the people in the Bible had Black skin, to include practically everyone in The Old Testament of the Bible. If Black skin was a curse from God, then Jesus was under the same curse. Ironically, Jesus was cursed, because of crucifixion.

LIE #2. Jesus was White.

TRUTH: Jesus was Jewish by birth and therefore a direct descendant of the Black men Solomon, David, Abraham, and Adam.

LIE #3. All Black Men Want White Women.

TRUTH: Many Black men still are unwilling to enter into an intimate relationship with a White woman, ironically, because of racism. "It's too easy for her to yell rape," is still the point of apprehension even in the year 2001.

LIE #4. All Black Men Have Large Penises.

TRUTH: During slavery in America, the master would place his wife on a pedestal, but sexual ravage the female slaves. Knowing that he was not satisfying his wife, and fearing she might take a slave out of spite, the White women were told that the Black man's penis was very large. It was hoped that this would frighten the White women enough to stop the entertainment of any thoughts of a sexual relationship with Black men. Penis size is not synonymous with skin color.

LIE #5. Most People in the Bible Are White.

TRUTH: The Old Testament of the Bible is a history of Black people, the origins of, and settings are the African continent. White people actually don't come into the picture in great numbers, until the first century Christians went forth to teach the Gospel to pagans, idol worshipers, and lost people of the world outside Africa.

LIE #6. African Tribes Started Slavery.

TRUTH: There may have always been some form of slavery, but the slavery that was unique to America, was started by the Whites of the Catholic Church, and continued until Abraham Lincoln used emancipation of the slaves in Rebel states as a tool to cripple the states in rebellion against the Union.

LIE #7. Egyptians Were White.

TRUTH: The ancient paintings of the tombs and pyramids of Egypt prove beyond a doubt that Egyptians are a Black people. The mummies themselves, their Black features, and modern Egyptians all prove the Blackness of Egypt.

LIE #8. Christianity is A White Religion.

TRUTH: True Christianity is not a religion of color, but a religion for all men who want to serve God in truth and spirit. Ironically Black people started Christianity, and the false White false religion, called Christianity which was foisted upon slaves by White masters was not, and is not Christianity at all.

LIE #9. (Black) People Evolved From Monkeys.

TRUTH: Though some brothers may resemble them, no animal has ever evolved into a man. The lack of necessary time needed for evolution from one life form to another, the lack of transitional fossils, and the inspired words of the Holy Bible all destroy the Theory of Evolution.

LIE #10. Black People rent as Intelligent as Whites.

TRUTH: Intelligence is not directly related to skin color. That which gives nonwhites the pigmentation is also found in brain cells. So if skin color did have anything to do with intelligence, nonwhites would be more intelligent. What have White people created that was not stolen from nonwhites? From the Airplane, to Zen Buddhism, and music in the middle, it was stolen from nonwhite cultures. The few things that can be remotely of expressly White origin are often not good. White people seem to have a corner on things such as hunting strictly for the pleasure of the hunt, swinging, and serial killing.

LIE #11. Adam and Eve were Caucasians.

TRUTH: We know that Adam and Eve were the original African people. They could in no way have been Caucasians, or have had Caucasian features.

LIE #12. Most Black People are on Welfare.

TRUTH: Statistics prove that the majority of people on Welfare are in fact White.

LIE #13. Black people Would Prefer Welfare to Work.

TRUTH: Sadly some may prefer welfare, but so too do some Whites. It is wrong to assume that all White or nonwhite would prefer Welfare to work.

LIE #14. Non-qualified Black People Get Jobs Because of Quotas.

TRUTH: How long would any business stay afloat if they hired non-qualified people to run their businesses? "No-brainer."

LIE #15. The First Black people in America Were Slaves.

TRUTH: The first Black people (Indians) were here before Whites and free, as were the Black people that came to America before and along with the Pilgrims.

LIE #16. Black People Started Masonry.

TRUTH: Not only was the false religion of Free Masonry started by Whites, but they then and still today do not wish fellowship as Masons with nonwhites. Hence the title Free and Accepted, or more correctly newly freed and accepted, or Black, as the first Blacks to follow Prince Hall were.

LIE #17. Malcolm X was Racist.

TRUTH: Malcolm in his early years reacted to racism leveled against Blacks, but in his last years of life was vehemently against racism, and for the brotherhood of all men without regard to the color of their skin.

LIE #18. Columbus Discovered America.

TRUTH: The Native Americans were here when Columbus landed, the Africans had been and gone, the Vikings had been and gone. To say Columbus discovered America is like saying, AI discovered your house while you were a resident there.

LIE #19. The Pilgrims and Founding Fathers Were Christians.

TRUTH: A Christian loves and desires for his neighbors what he desires for himself. A Christian does not commit genocide, and a Christian does not swindle ignorant people. "Nuff said?"

LIE #20. The Civil War Was Fought Over Slavery.

TRUTH: The Civil War was over the southern states having the power to govern themselves and slavery was only part of the whole, leading to the Civil War. It was not singly to free the slave and Lincoln did not want to free any slaves, much less all of them. The former president was willing to maintain slavery or end it to save the Union.

LIE #21. Abraham Lincoln Freed All Slaves

TRUTH: Abraham Lincolns Emancipation Proclamation called for the freeing of only the slaves in the states still in rebellion to the North.

LIE #22. The Non-Violent Movement of Sixties Won Civil Rights for Blacks

TRUTH: Blacks actually enjoyed civil rights when they arrived in America along with the pilgrims, and after the Civil War, but necessary changes to recoup our rights as citizens of America only occurred when Black people showed that they were willing to stand up in self-defense.

How to Change the World

A merica claims that the use of the atomic bomb at Hiroshima and Nagasaki stopped the war and saved the lives of thousands of people, (by killing many non-military people)! Likewise, when the Black people in the south began to defend themselves against the violence of White people, the president sent troops in, and passed civil rights legislation! The American Revolution led to freedom and certain rights for the revolutionaries. Likewise, merely the beginnings of a true Black revolution drove this United States of America to make laws granting civil/human rights to all of its members. Some White Americans are so afraid of Black revolution that merely seeing a group of Black men together is uncomfortable to them. Black students are encouraged to mingle with White students. American soldiers are given direct orders not to appear to form clicks, and Black Army Basic Trainees are punished for grouping themselves together. The fear of violent revolution is enough to force America to do right. Since it has been historically proven that violence works, why should we attempt to acquire for ourselves that which others have acquired by another method, when history has given us a method that works.

When Dr. King phoned then President, Kennedy to ask for help in the defense of Black people, the president said he could do nothing basically because it was a matter under state versus federal jurisdiction. When Black people began to defend themselves against their attackers, then the president sent in federal troops to aid Whites who were now receiving their just due for the violence they had been inflicting on the Blacks. Since history clearly shows that people usually do not gain freedom, justice, and equality without the shedding of blood, I believe Dr. King would have moved naturally from his path of passive nonviolence. An all-out violent revolution against the United States would have, of course, been fool hardy, but I sincerely believe that it was the Black man's defending himself that lead to the freedom we have in America today.

Mahdi, rightfully guided being. "What is right?" Like truth, right is that which is proper, and correct, whether it is known and accepted, or not. How would the White world react to a Black Mahdi? My stated goals were translated into a disdainful phrase, but unlike the young Malcolm Little, I will not be driven off course. Unlike Martin Luther King, Jr., I will not spend my time striving to make a dream reality, when history has absolutely given the correct answers. I of course, rejected that doctor's diagnosis, and I want to believe that there are more good White people than bad, but he is added to the list of at least questionable. What am I as a Black man to think of a White man who would say that my desire to change the world is a delusion?

I also added him to the list of people who, by their negative response to my goals, would help me obtain them. All great achievers had a slew of people in their life that told them they could not do this or that. Seeing that I share many of the traits and commonalties of past achievers, I know that I need only persevere for my success to be assured. I have learned that the people who have achieved greatness in their fields have all had certain things in common:

Like Mahalia Jackson, they were told "You can't." Like Frank Sinatra, they were told to "Stop dreaming." Like Elvis Presley, they were told, "You will never be anything." Like Colonel Sanders, they were told to, "You are too old." Like Ray Krock, they were told, "That does not work." Many others with dreams and goals were told, if God meant it to be . . . I say, the world can be made better, and God did mean it to be! It was God, who said of the Tower of Babel, "Look, man has made a mighty work, <u>if they come together, there is nothing man cannot accomplish</u>." I will take the word of God, over the word of man every day of my life.

Why would someone say I have delusions of grandeur when I give a clear and acceptable explanation of how I, united with others, intend to change the world? It is only a delusion if it is impossible. Uniting Blacks may be improbable, but not impossible. Furthermore, if I say am going to then you cannot say what will not happen in the future unless it is currently impossible, but how many things have we been able to do in just the last ten to fifteen years that were before then considered impossible?

CHAPTER EIGHTEEN

How We Can Destroy Racism

Cicely Tyson's character in the TV series "The Women of Brewster's Place" said, "Black isn't beautiful, Black isn't ugly, Black is just Black."

Powerful words that shout out that there nothing inherently good or evil about the color of one's skin; one is simply a color, period. A person chooses to be good or evil regardless of what he or she looks like. As such, the steps necessary to correct problems usually have very little to do with skin color.

The general plan for overcoming almost any problem can be obtained by filling in the template below. As stated in the beginning of this book, I do not claim to have all the answers. I can only offer my ideas, and through implementation and communication, we can together find the final answers. I think there are some questions that can only be answered by racists. Why do you hate? and possibly, what can be done to turn that hate into love? To say it is only because of my color, will not fit into the equation for change. Therefore we can deduce that color alone, is not the real problem. We must get honest answers to effect a real change.

To solve any problem, one must merely fill in the following:

PROBLEM	SOLVER
Identify the Problem	
Gather Information	
List Possible Courses of Action	
Select Best Course of Action	
Make a Plan	
Initiate Plan	
Evaluate Progress	
Make Necessary Changes to Plan	
Initiate Corrected Plan	
Reevaluate Progress	

To solve the problem of racism:

1. Identify what the actual cause of racism is.
2. Communicate to determine what can be done to accept or correct the cause of racism.
3. Speak in clear unclouded terms so there are no misunderstandings.
4. Good people of all races must take a vocal and active stand against all forms of prejudice and racism.
5. Black people must stop being niggers! (It is not the dip in your walk, the filth in our talk, or the unique way we wear clothes that make us Black!) We can not give justification to White racism by our ignorant acts of violence, unintelligent speech, and unlearned behavior; this is our part in ending racism.
6. Prosecution to the fullest extent of the law, those persons who are found guilty of hate crimes! When the fear of the law is brought back, men will respect and keep the law!

CHAPTER NINETEEN

Closing

In the movie: <u>Meet John Doe</u>, a man threatens to commit suicide if society does not change, and they changed. If this were reality, not enough caring people would unite to stop that suicide. If the loss of life could make this world better, I would consider the position myself, but one man far greater than I, has given his life for mankind, unfortunately for some, to no avail.

All I can do at this point is offer my humble ideas of what I believe will work, and starting with the man in the mirror, challenge the world to prove me right or wrong by implementing my ideas. I have rolled up my sleeves and I am doing my part daily, what have you done for the betterment of the world you live in? I challenge you, Americans of all shades to rise up and be the great nation you claim to be!

APPENDIX

As the author of this important work, it is my sincerest hope and prayer that the reader:

1. Will not take me as one who thinks he knows everything, I do not.
2. Has kept an open mind while reading this book.
3. Will implement the principles espoused.
4. Strive to better his or herself and the world around him or her.
5. Will contact me with the desire of correcting any error I may have made and working with myself and others to correct the problems of the world. It can be done.
6. Will share this work and others I have produced with others.

Thank you for purchasing this book.-Tony DeVaun McNeil

It's a burden all right. But AIDS isn't the greatest burden I have had to bear . . . Being Black is the greatest burden I've had to bear. -Arthur Ashe

Races, faces, where your butt comes from, is where your space is. I've seen the bright get duller, I'm not gonna spend my life being a color!
Black or White -Michael Jackson

Truth is that which is accurate, whether it is known or not, accepted or not, and truth is that which is, whether it is proven or not.-Tony D. McNeil

He who knows not, and knows not he knows not is foolish, shun him. He who knows not, and knows he knows not is simple, teach him. He who knows not, and knows not he knows not is asleep, awaken him. He who knows and knows he knows, is wise, follow him. - Bruce Lee

Black is beautiful when it is a slum kid studying to enter college, when it is a man learning new skills for a new job, or a slum mother battling to give her kids a chance for a better life. But white is beautiful, too, when it helps change society to make our system work for black people also. White is ugly when it oppresses blacks-and so is black ugly when black people exploit other blacks. No race has a monopoly on vice or virtue, and the worth of an individual is not related to the color of his skin.-Whitney M. Young Jr.

When your enemy says, I'm only looking out for you, look out!
-Tony DeVaun McNeil

"Thank God I am black. White people will have a lot to answer for at the last judgment."- Bishop Desmond Tutu

"Proper planning and perseverance especially and in spite of minor or gross failure leads to eventual success if you never quit." -Tony DeVaun McNeil

www.ingramcontent.com/pod-product-compliance
Lightning Source LLC
Chambersburg PA
CBHW030221140626
46545CB00011B/704